TURN
WISHES
TO WINS

Common Sense Guide To Uncommon Results

BY

ANNE ATULAEGWU

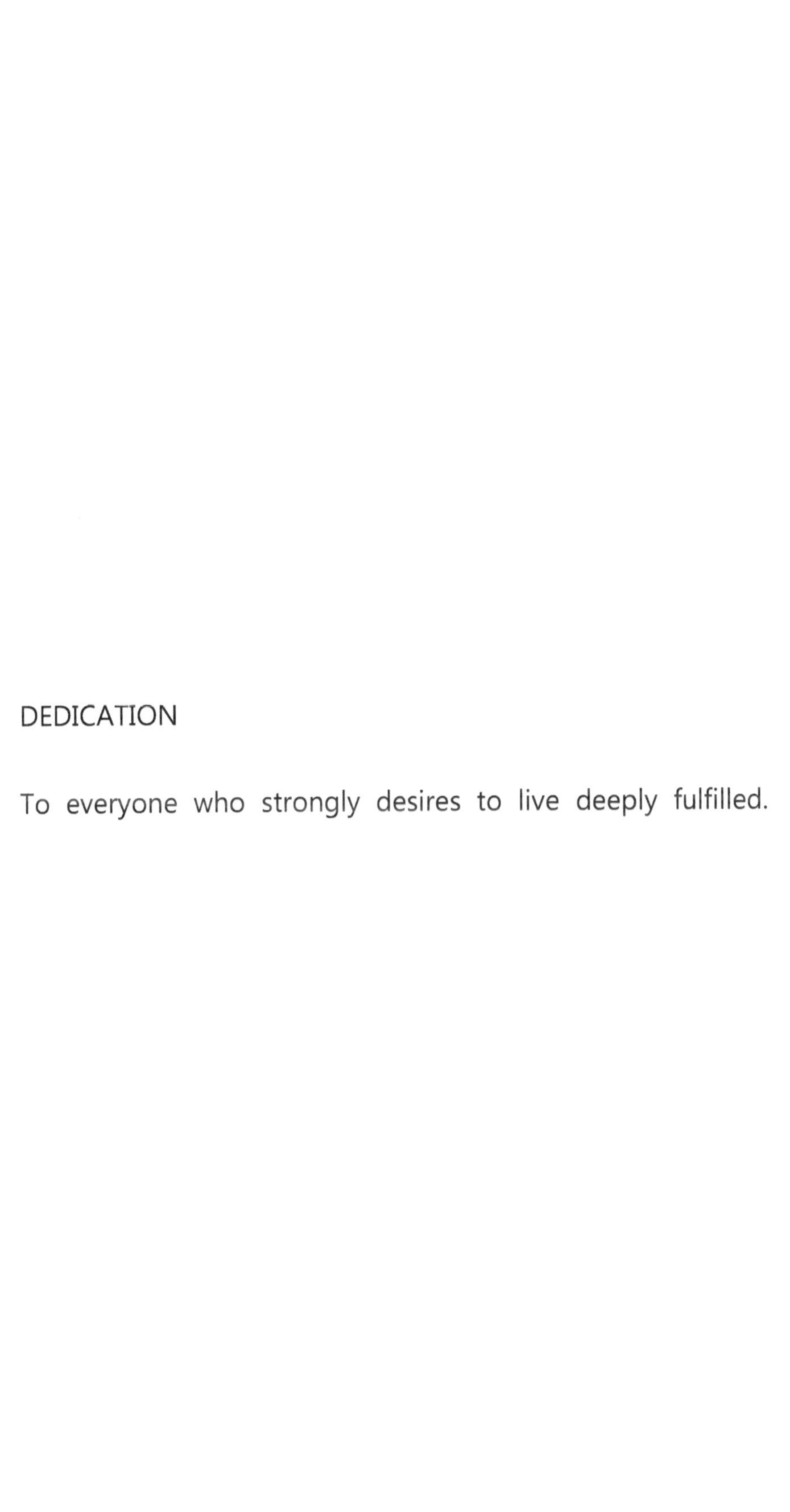

DEDICATION

To everyone who strongly desires to live deeply fulfilled.

CONTENTS

INTRODUCTION

When I was younger, I had a wish.

I wished that I could move from street to street selling to anyone who cared to buy. I admired people who moved about carrying their wares on their heads because I felt they had the privilege of sightseeing and freedom of movement.

The only chance I got to see places was when we were in the car on our way to church or school. The other times were when we occasionally visited Amusement Park or stopped by the then famous Mr. Biggs for lunch. This was in the 90's.

I soon got bored from seeing the same routes and sights. I wished for more sightseeing opportunities and freedom of movement. I thought the only way I could get those was to be like the other children or adults who hawked their wares.

One day, my wish came to be!

My mum came across bananas sold unbelievably cheap. She bought a lot and decided to sell some of it. She got home from work that day and asked that I took the bananas to her friend's store some streets away.

My eyes dilated in excitement. I couldn't curtail my happiness. My mum never knew why I was so excited about the task. If only she knew I intended to hawk those bananas on my way to her friend's store.

I set the tray of bananas on my head and I began my walk to the store when suddenly, I had mixed feelings. I felt shame. I wondered if people would think we were suddenly poor. I wondered what they would think about me. I began to feel uneasy.

Where did all the excitement go? I thought that this was what I desperately wanted. I even remember praying that I would one day hawk like those kids and adults that I admired. Why don't I feel as great as I thought I would?

I walked on, hoping someone would buy from me. Perhaps, the excitement would return when I made a sale. Sadly, no one bought from me until I arrived at mum's friend's store.

I greeted the lady and her clients and on her authorization, I displayed my bananas in front of her store. The excitement returned as I thought, "Here I was finally selling something on the street". That excitement was short-lived as the mixed feelings returned almost immediately.

"What if my school mates drove by? What if a

member of our church saw me? What if someone who knew my parents saw me? What would they think? I began to worry and couldn't enjoy the moment.

Why was I ashamed? Wasn't this what I wanted all my life? At least, I had seen new places in the neighborhood and I am finally selling something.

I sat there worrying the whole time and wondering why I wasn't as excited about my "wish come true", as I was when I nursed the desire in my heart.

The day came to an end with only two sales. I was disappointed. How could I sell only two bunches of bananas on a Saturday, from morning till evening? Was this what those hawkers experienced daily? I went home sad and was glad my mum never asked me to do that again.

I learnt from that experience and several others that wishes come true. Some of them, you have to intentionally pursue and others like my street hawk experience, life makes happen for you.

However, whether you intentionally pursue your wishes or life makes them happen, I have found that true satisfaction and deep fulfillment isn't dependent on the manifestation of a wish. Rather, it is dependent on how clear you are about what you wish for and why you wish for it.

For instance, a lady could spend all her time strongly chasing marriage only to eventually get married and realize she just wanted financial security and someone (a child) to call her mum but not the weight and wins of a marriage.

wanted the privilege of going wherever I desired without having to worry about my parents' approval. I wanted to know my neighbourhood and see more interesting places around. I thought hawking goods was my best chance at that. I finally got my wish and had a horrible day because it turned out that hawking, freedom and sightseeing were not exactly related.

Turn wishes to wins book is not another magic wand formula to a made-in-heaven life. No one has the magic wand formula. Most books or courses that promise that actually never deliver because there really isn't any magic wand formula to your dream life. This is because we all want different things from life.

However, there is one thing we all want from life. Children want it, adults want it, grieving wives want it, disrespected husbands want it, failing students want it, A-list students want it, the poor want it, the rich want it, the divorced want it, the singles want it, the married wants it, professionals want it, applicants want it, and you want it. It is called **deep, lasting fulfillment**.

Fulfillment is the achievement of something desired, promised or predicted[1].
You may have no promises to look forward to, you may have no predictions to anticipate, but there is no second in your life that you are without a desire.

From simple every day matters such as desiring sleep, desiring food, desiring acceptance and recognition, to the important milestone matters such as desiring a spouse, desiring a degree
desiring a huge income, desiring a successful ministry, desiring a global business; there is no time in your life, when

you are without desires.

Desires are the roots of all wishes and how you handle your desires determine if you have wins or losses in life. Read that line again.

In the first part of this book (rule storms), I show you how to navigate the 5 most common and deadly storms of life. These storms challenge your desires, incapacitate your wishes and prevent you from recording the wins that you deserve.

In the second part (execute missions), I show you the 8 powers upon and by which every notable result is built. You will be equipped to execute your missions effectively and excellently. No more regrets, No more wasted resources, no more misplaced priorities, No more buried hopes.

In the third part (Grab gold), I share with you 7 qualities of people who turn wishes into wins. Never again would you worry that the good you deserve is yet to manifest because you will become someone who knows how to turn wishes into wins and live unapologetically fulfilled.

Let's get you started on your best life yet.

Committed to your fulfillment
Princess-Anne Atulaegwu

RULE STORMS

RULE STORMS

You got to be willing to walk in a storm.
Ray Lewis

You learn to know a pilot in a storm.
Lucius Annaeus Seneca

If you want to see the sunshine, you have to weather the storm.
Frank Lane

He only earns his freedom and his life who takes them every day by storm.
Johann Wolfgang von Goethe

If you spend your whole life waiting for the storm, you will never enjoy the sunshine. **Morris west**

The fishermen know that the sea is dangerous and the storm terrible, but they have never found these dangers sufficient reason for remaining ashore.
Vincent Van Gogh

Remember, the storm is a good opportunity for the pine and the cypress to show their strength and their stability. **HoChi Minh**

I pass my life in preventing the storm from blowing down the tent and I drive in the pegs as fast as they are pulled up. **Abraham Lincoln**

When something is important enough, you do it even if the odds are not in your favour. **Elon Musk**

Every storm has a hidden rudder beneath the fuss. Calmly find the rudder and you will wield the storm in your favour. **Anne Atulaegwu**

Never cut a tree down in the wintertime. Never make a negative decision in the low time. Never make your most important decisions when you are in your worst moods. Wait. Be patient. The storm will pass. The spring will come. **Robert Schuller**

A head full of fears has no space for dreams. **Unknown**

Worry pretends to be necessary but serves no useful purpose. **Eckhart Tole**

Nothing diminishes anxiety faster than action. **Walter Anderson**

Let whatever you do today be enough. **Unknown**

1

FEAR

Limits like fear is often an illusion- Michael Jordan

Conquering Fear (An Ethiopian Folktale)

Once upon a time in an Ethiopian village, there lived a boy who was so shy and fearful of the world around him that his family called him Miobe, frightened one.
"Why do you call me that?" the boy asked his grandfather. The old man laughed. "Because you are afraid," he answered. The boy's grandmother, his mother, his father and the neighbors said the same thing.

Miobe pondered these words and decided he must find a way to conquer fear, and that night when everyone was fast asleep, he packed a sack and set off into the world to find out what he feared and to conquer it.

That night he slept under the wide umbrella of sky and stared up at the darkness. Before drifting off, he whispered to himself, "I see you, but I will conquer you, fear."

He fell asleep wrapped in his blanket, but at midnight the wolves began to howl.

The sound woke Miobe, but instead of running away, he walked toward the sound, saying aloud, "I will conquer you, fear."

He walked until the sun began to rise, and when he saw its golden orb, he smiled with relief, for he had survived the first night. "I am becoming brave," he said as he walked on.

Soon he came to a village, and for a moment he thought, "I don't know these people at all. They might be unkind to a stranger." But he straightened up and walked right into the village, saying aloud, "I will conquer you, fear."

He walked into the village square, and there he found the village elders gathered, muttering among themselves. As Miobe came near, they looked up and sneered, "Who are you?"

"I'm traveling the world to become brave," Miobe answered.

The elders laughed. "Fool! No one can find bravery where it does not exist."

"What do you mean?" Miobe asked. The elders sighed unhappily. "We are finished," said one old man. "Our village

is being threatened by a monster up on the mountain."
Miobe followed the old man's gaze to the top of the
mountain.

"See him, there," the old man said.

Miobe squinted. He did not want to insult the man, but he
saw nothing there.

"Look," said another man. "See? It has the head of a
crocodile. A monstrous crocodile!"

"And his body is as horrible as a hippopotamus. A gigantic
hippopotamus!"

"It's like a dragon!" another man cried, "with fire shooting
from its snout!"

Now Miobe began to see the monster. He began to see the
smoke and fire, the wrinkled skin, the fiery eyes. "I see," he
said, but silently he promised himself he would not be afraid.
So he walked away from the elders, into the main parts of
the village.

Everywhere people cowered. The little children hid inside,
refusing to go to school. "If the children go outside," the
women said, "the monster will come down from the
mountain and eat them. Everyone knows monsters eat
children."

The farmers hovered inside their doorways, hoes and rakes
in hand; outside their horses stood unharnessed. "We cannot
work," they told Miobe. "If we go into the fields, the monster
will come down and get us."

Miobe saw wandering goats, sheep and cows out at the
edge of the village, but no one came to milk the animals or

tend to them. No one planted crops. Few left their homes, preferring to hide indoors.

"The monster is as big as 10 barges!" they whispered among themselves as Miobe listened. "The monster is going to destroy us!"

Finally Miobe decided it was up to him to destroy the monster. "I wish to conquer fear," he announced, "and so I shall go slay the monster!"

"No, son, don't do it!" the elders cried. Mothers gathered to try to shield the young man from harm. Fathers shook their heads and warned, "You will die."
Miobe shivered and his heart fluttered, but he was determined. "I must conquer fear!" he said, and he set off.

At the base of the mountain, he looked up and felt a chill of fear run down his spine. That monster looked even bigger and fierier than any dragon, fiercer than a whole pack of wolves or a nest of snakes. He remembered the days when he had been afraid. He took a deep breath and began to climb. As he climbed, he looked up, but now he saw the monster seemed to be growing smaller. "How peculiar," he said aloud. "My eyes are deceiving me." He continued to climb.

When he was halfway up, he looked again. He squinted, shielding his eyes, but the monster's eyes no longer seemed so fierce, and the flames no longer shot from its snout.
"The closer I get, the smaller he looks," Miobe said puzzlingly. He continued to climb, though now he pulled his dagger from his sack so that he would be prepared.

As he came around a bend in the path, he saw the summit before him. He gasped. The monster had disappeared.

Miobe turned and looked behind him. Surely the creature was going to sneak up from behind to attack. But when he turned, he saw nothing. He heard nothing. He held his breath. He looked left. He looked right. He continued to climb. At long last he reached the summit and all was empty and quiet. Nothing was there.

Suddenly he heard a sound at his feet. He looked down and saw a little creature, just like a toad with wrinkled skin and round, frightened eyes.

He bent down and picked it up. "Who are you?" he asked. "How did you become so small?" But the monster said nothing, and so he cradled it in his hand and walked down the mountain.

When he reached the village, the people cried, "He's safe!" and they surrounded him.

Miobe held out his hand and showed them the tiny wrinkled toad. "This is the monster," he said.

"What is your name?" asked the elder. The creature croaked, and the elder looked up at the crowd and said, "Miobe has brought us the monster. Its name is fear."

** ** **

Fear not little flock, it is your Father's good pleasure to give you the kingdom- Luke 12:32 (NIV)
Fear ye not, For ye are of more value than many sparrows. Mathew 10:31(NIV)

Fear is a feeling **induced by perceived** danger or threat that occurs in certain types of organisms, which causes a change in metabolic and organ functions and ultimately a change in behavior, such as fleeing, hiding, or freezing from **perceived** traumatic events.[1]

While what we fear might be real or imagined, fear as an emotion is often a product of perception.

Perception is the way in which something is regarded, understood, or interpreted.[2]

It is how we interpret an experience or exposure that heightens or expels the emotion of fear.

Fear is a distressing emotion aroused by impending danger, evil, pain, whether the threat is real or imagined; It is the feeling or condition of being afraid.[3]

LET'S HEAR WHAT FAMOUS PEOPLE
HAVE TO SAY ABOUT FEAR.

"Fears are nothing more than states of mind." -Napoleon Hill (Author of Think And Grow Rich)

"It's OK to get butterfly in your stomach; the key is to learn how to make them fly in formation." -Georges St-Pierre (UFC Welterweight Champion

"There was never any fear for me, no fear of failure. If I miss a shot, so what? I've missed more than 9000 shots in my career, I've lost more than 300 games, 26 times I've been trusted to take the game winning shot and missed. I've failed over and over in my life, and that's why I succeed." –Michael Jordan (Retired NBA player- in case you didn't know!

"Inaction breeds doubt and fear. Action breeds confidence and courage. If you want to conquer fear, do not sit home and think about it. Go out and get busy." –Dale Carnegie (Author of How To Make Friends & Win Influence)

"What developed in my early days was the attitude to start attacking the thing I was scared of". –Will Smith (Actor & Singer)

TWO KINDS OF FEAR

<u>Rational:</u> Fear that is based on clear thought or reason. It protects you. An example is the fear of wild animals such as Lion, Tiger, Cheetah. You definitely don't want to mess with those guys (Laughs).

<u>Irrational:</u> Fear that isn't based on thinking and is unreasonable. It prevents you. It holds you back from fully embracing the riches that life offers.
An example is the fear of intimacy with others.

HOW TO DEAL WITH FEAR

There are two approaches to dealing with fear.
These approaches are applicable to different situations.

-Fear Mastery
-Fear Extinguishment

Fear Mastery refers to control or superiority over fear. Example of an area where you need fear mastery is public speaking.

HOW TO MASTER FEAR

IDENTIFY the fear

What are you afraid of? Could it be rejection? Being Misunderstood? Failure? Fear of selling to people? Fear of the Dark? Fear of the unknown or the future?

DETACH yourself

By this I mean you should separate yourself from the picture of the fear in your heart. Think about it like a movie. I cry profusely when seeing a movie that appeals to my emotions. The only time I am able to stop crying when I see movies like that, is to remind myself that it is just a movie. You are not your emotions/feelings. Feelings are products of thoughts and beliefs. This consciousness will help you control your thoughts and gain mastery over fear.

DECOLOUR the fear

Take the aliveness in your negative imagination away by imagining that the opposite of your fear happened.

DECORATE your hope
Imagine the good happening by adding realistic features like a date, time, place and colour. Dwell on it and enjoy the liveliness of your hope.

ENGAGE your hope
Start doing what you need to do to create your dream/hope. For instance, if you are afraid of poverty? You could learn and start a business and move towards a financially flourishing life.

Fear Extinguishment:
This refers to completely snuffing out fear from your heart. Example of an area where you need fear extinguishment is in fear of the unknown or fear of the future.

HOW TO EXTINGUISH FEAR

IDENTIFY the fear
Just as we discussed earlier

CONNECT with Christ
Connecting with Christ is as simple as Romans 10:9 directs.
If you declare with your mouth, "Jesus is Lord," and believe in your heart that God raised him from the dead, you will be saved. (NIV)
There is a level of boldness and steel confidence that comes from being connected to Christ.
That connection supplies your spirit with all that you need to

enjoy a life of endless possibilities amidst storms.

ENGAGE the power at work within you

*"His divine power has given us everything we need for a godly life **through our knowledge of him** who called us by his own glory and goodness."* 2 peter 1:3(NIV)

Do you really know Jesus
Do you know his strength and awesome power?
Have you encountered the recklessness of his love?
Do you know how faithful He is and has been to you?
It is what you know about the person and personality of Christ that gives you confidence to go through life unhindered, unfurled by storms.

MY GREATEST FEAR EXPELLER

Beyond Psychology, I consider Psalm 23 the greatest fear expeller and perfect fear recipe. Let's see the New Living Translation below

The LORD is my shepherd;
I have all that I need.
He lets me rest in green meadows;
he leads me beside peaceful streams.
He renews my strength.
He guides me along right paths,
bringing honor to his name.

*Even when I walk
through the darkest valley,
I will not be afraid,
for you are close beside me.
Your rod and your staff
protect and comfort me.
You prepare a feast for me
in the presence of my enemies.
You honor me by anointing my head with oil.
My cup overflows with blessings.
Surely your goodness and unfailing love will pursue me
all the days of my life,
and I will live in the house of the LORD
forever.*

That was written by a boy who had come face to face with a Lion and Beer. (1 Samuel 17:37)

A boy who defeated a giant when grown men hid behind rocks. (1 Samuel 17:37)

A boy who feared for his life such that he pretended to be mad. (1 Samuel 21:13)

A boy who had seen hunger days when he went in search of food for himself and the others dependent on him
(1 Samuel 25)

A man who had felt the fear of the loss of a child and did lose the child. (2 Samuel 12:16)

A man who fought many battles against countless soldiers.

David clearly, had been there, seen it all and even won the T-shirt. He definitely knew what He was saying when he shared Psalms 23 with us. Like David I have made the Lord my shepherd therefore I have all I need to fearlessly live fulfilled and unapologetically so too. Have you made the Lord your Shepherd?

If you haven't there is a quick guide for you just after the last chapter of this book. Flip there to make the Lord your shepherd.

THE ONLY FEAR YOU ARE PERMITTED TO HAVE

The fear of the Lord leads to life: Then one rests content, untouched by trouble. Proverbs 19:23 (NIV)

I remember my high school days at Evangel College. I dreaded being caned by the mathematics teacher called, Mr. Madu. The skill by which he drops that stick on an ass could make one stand for days. I wasn't a rebellious student but there could be occasions of mass punishment which I feared and often prayed wouldn't happen.

The fear of Mr. Madu made us listen attentively in class, solve mathematics and further mathematics assignments and not turn our necks when he was invigilating. Unconsciously, we became used to behaving in mathematics class at least. (Laughs)

However, the kind of fear God seeks is not the kind we had for Mr. Madu. The fear of Mr. Madu made us sit up only in mathematics class. We did not take the "attitude" into other classes because that fear didn't change us.

God desires and deserves the fear of His person and deep

appreciation for his wisdom such that we are led to make choices that please Him. This kind of fear brings lasting transformation on our lives.

Proverbs says the fear of the Lord leads to life. When you have fear (awesome reverence) for God, his person and principles, you would enjoy LIFE-the vitality, fruitfulness and fulfillment of existence.

God wants to lead you into LIFE. He wants to help you rest content (in satisfaction) and untouched by trouble. Have respect for his instruction. Stop being afraid of popular opinion. FEAR GOD; FEEL LIFE!

WHAT IT REALLY MEANS TO FEAR THE LORD

See Psalms 34:7-10 (NKJV)

The angel of the Lord encampeth
Round about them that fear him, and delivereth them.
O taste and see that the Lord is good:
Blessed is the man that trusteth in him.
O fear the Lord, ye his saints:
For there is no want to them that fear him.
The young lions do lack, and suffer hunger:
But they that seek the Lord shall not want any good thing.

The fear of the lord entails being so in tune with the heart of God that you become sensitive to his will, his ways and his word. I happen to have a REAL relationship with the person of CHRIST (Ever grateful for that) and so I find myself being conscious of his feelings. He has emotions and so I commit to obeying his instruction from scripture and personal revelation; not only because it is for my good as seen in the above scripture but because I really care about his feelings. That is what it means to fear the Lord.

WHAT IS IN THE FEAR OF GOD FOR YOU?

With the fear of God comes several benefits as seen below;

<u>The angel of God encampeth around you and delivers you from Satan and his agents.</u>
Some years ago, some robbers came to our street. They robbed a young man, took off all electronics in his apartment. They came to ours while we slept and they cut open the padlocks on our gates (both entrances). I heard the sound of a falling metal but I never knew we were about to be raided. Though they cut open the padlocks, the gate never opened and they never went in. I wondered what stopped them. It must have been an angel of the Lord.

<u>You shall lack no good thing.</u>
Here, it got specific. You shall lack NO GOOD THING. God meets needs. He meets mine. He will meet yours. No want means No LACK.

Would you dare to walk in the fear of God?
Rather than fear hunger, losing a boyfriend or sugar mum and dad, some cash or popularity? All those won't protect you nor GENUINELY and UNCONDITIONALLY care for you

like JESUS DOES FOR HIS OWN.

FEAR GOD; FEEL LOVE!

2

WANED EXCITEMENT

Character is the ability to carry out a good resolution long after the excitement of the moment has passed-Cavett Robert

This storm is subtle but powerful. Often, people begin projects, relationships, pursuits with lots of zest but half way down the road, they can't find the passion or excitement with which they started. Waned excitement is responsible for the death of many dreams, relationship with God and spouses.

Can you remember one time you abandoned something

dear because you just couldn't feel the vibe anymore? Perhaps you started writing a book and excitement ebbed off or you attended training and left the hall swearing you were going to start the business the next day only to wake up and not find the zeal?

There are no general rules for restoring waned excitement because the approach for restoring excitement in a romantic relationship isn't the same for restoring excitement on a project, your job, ministry or life generally. I'm therefore going to focus on specific areas that I can confidently help you win in.

DEALING WITH WANED EXCITEMENT OVER A PROJECT

Let's assume you've just started working on your new album, your thesis or writing a book but can't find the excitement or passion with which you began. Here is what to do

Take a mental break
Stop working on that thing. Take some time out to relax. Get some sleep, hang out with friends, watch TV or go for a massage.

Work on something else
I'm sure your life doesn't revolve around that project. Now is the time to do other things that really matter to you. If your project was related to figures, avoid anything figure related. If it's about a certain music, listen to a different kind of music. This deliberate distraction will spur your mind to relax

and get more creative when you return to the project.

Share with others

Be wise about who you choose to talk about your project with. Look out for people who are genuinely interested in your wellbeing and believe in your project. They could show you a new perspective that may fire up excitement and commitment required for you to accomplish your project.

Chunk down

Waned excitement sometimes happen because you feel overwhelmed. Instead of trying to swallow the Elephant at one breakfast sitting, it is okay to cut it in pieces, preserve and schedule to eat during breakfast over a convenient period of time.

Be creative

Creativity may mean that you relocate temporarily. If you used to work in your bedroom, try the living room. If that doesn't work for you, go on a vacation to a friend's house over the weekend or spend one or two nights in an affordable hotel. This can help reset your mind and create excitement as you work on your project in a new, comfortable environment.

DEALING WITH WANED EXCITEMENT OVER YOUR RELATIONSHIP WITH GOD

Femi pulled the car by the side. They had driven too far to

return to the Adetola's when the tyre went flat on Ozamba drive.

"What do we do, babe?" He asked Shola.

Shola wasn't in the mood to respond to her husband. It has been weeks since they last had a meaningful conversation and this wasn't the moment in which she wants to neither answer questions nor make suggestions.

"Babe" Femi called again. This time, reaching for her arm.

Shola shrugged her arm off his soft grip and looked out the window.

Dead silence struck the car.

It was 1 am in the morning and they had no spare tyre available. Frustrated but calm, Femi placed his head on the steering and prayed silently.

"Father, I married Shola because I love her and in moments like this, I will want her to talk with me even if she has no solution. Please soften her heart towards me ".

Shola opened the door and stepped out in the dark. She was just going to keep walking until ....

Frightened for his wife, Femi jumped out right after her. "Babe, I miss you. Why are you being cold towards me? "He asked with tears in his eyes.

He wasn't sure whether the car or his wife's attitude was the right priority. He just knew He couldn't continue to endure the cold between them.

Looking intently into his eyes, Shola said, "I just don't feel like I love you anymore."

Those words dropped like moulded bean balls in boiling oil – sleek, fast and festering all at once. Femi couldn't reconcile those words with the history he shared with Shola.

They met as teenagers while at Irekpodo high school in Ondo south of Nigeria. Shola had been his first and only love and after eight years of dating, two years of engagement and three of marriage, he couldn't comprehend what she meant by " I just don't feel like I love you anymore"

Femi fell on his knees, soaked in tears already. He begged Shola to please stop as her attitude was shredding him like minced meat.

Shola looked away. She couldn't bear to see the man she once loved, kneeling in front of her but she knew she wanted something new. She was tired of being with the same person. She wanted an adventure that Segun, her new boss appeared to offer. She just didn't want to keep being with the same man. She was bored.

**** ** ****

Many dynamics come into play when boy meets girl and both dance to a vow. It's easy to feel empathy for Femi because we can see no sane reason for Shola to act this way to her lover of thirteen solid years just because a boss showed up.

It is also apparent that what is missing between Femi and Shola is sound communication. Shola is supposed to tell Femi what her boss does that she likes and Femi is supposed to make a few adjustments to bring those sparks into their relationship right? Well, that is easier said than done.

The one thing which prevents effective communication in a relationship is the fear of rejection. Like any normal person,

Shola must have feared that mentioning her boss (Segun) to Femi could bring distrust. She doesn't want Femi to see her as unfaithful and she also doesn't want the fun she is enjoying with Segun to stop. Her mind has been powerfully influenced by Segun's presence and acts of "love" that she has began to see her husband as boring. Like Shola, most people don't remember that vows are made for moments like this.

Just before we judge Shola, let's take a sincere look into our lives. I speak to believers at this point. You fell in love with a man (Christ) years ago. You enjoyed his presence. You were content with any and everything He provided and what He was yet to provide was no problem because you knew He would eventually do. Then years have rolled by, and facets of life flaunt their charm before your eyes. The allure of international recognition, the fragrance of fame, the relish of world approval and the craving of ambition has stealthily began to pull your heart out of sync with the one you once vowed to love.

At the beginning, we would do anything for him. We would go anywhere for him. We would give anything for him.
But now...
His promises appear impossible.
He appears to drag his feet in fulfilling his word.
We have become bored reading his letters- Romans sounds roll mats and we will rather read fables than his word.

What did Femi do to deserve Shola's change of heart? I guess you will say nothing.
Looking inward, what has the Lord done to deserve your

misplaced affection?

Femi could misunderstand Shola if she opened up about her new distraction but unlike man, Christ doesn't misunderstand.

He's walked the earth and he knows what it feels to not have enough money, not have a spouse to hold at night, to not be recognized on global television just because your opinion doesn't tally with the rest of the world's. However, He was committed to his course. Commitment is the essence of vows. **Vows are made in feel good times for when passion wanes.**

HERE IS WHAT TO DO

Remember your first love
What where the things you did at the start when you got saved? Start doing them again even if you don't feel like it. Intercede for people, talk to them about Jesus, and wake up early like you used to, to spend time with God.

Be honest
Tell the lord how you feel. Tell him how bored you feel and ask him to rekindle your love for him and his presence. He won't be mad, he will help. Talk to him about the distractions and let him rekindle the warmth of the love you both shared when you first believed.

Pray in tongues
Praying in tongues also known as praying in the spirit

energizes your spirit. You will definitely come alive and feel renewed when you do. To learn more about tongue speaking, go to the resource page of https://www.birthplaceministries.org

The Lord awaits your return with open arms. He loves you so much and can't wait to bathe you in the kisses of his undying love.

DEALING WITH WANED EXCITEMENT OVER LIFE

Life can gradually feel boring especially during grief. Times when living feels like chore and every day activities begin to choke are clear signs that you may be experiencing waned excitement over life. The following actions would help.

<u>Speak with God</u>
People underestimate talk therapy. It isn't only humans who listen when we speak, God listens too.
Go on a date to a park, a pizza outlet (my favourite) or book one night at a lodge centre or hotel and intentionally invite God over. Pretend that you can see Him and tell Him how you feel.
I can't explain it, but times when I did this I felt like he literally embraced me. Nothing in this world can compare to the warmth and comfort you will feel and when God wraps his arms around you. Give it a try, honey.

<u>Create an achievement/victory/gratitude Jar</u>
I call this the amnesia therapy. It is possible to forget your

lofty and little achievements within a short time frame. To help you remember, relive and enjoy the good feeling that comes with your achievements, create and keep an achievement jar.

Simply buy sticky notes or any multi coloured writing pad and on each sheet, write out your achievement in the last one year or more. Fold them individually and toss them in a see through jar where the colours can pop at you. From time to time, open the jar and read one each day. It will inspire you to enjoy life, seeing that you have done good so far.

Keep in mind that your achievement doesn't have to be as grand as being the president of your country. It could be something as "little" but insanely significant as volunteering in an organization you admire, finally buying that pair of jean, forgiving Jane or Joe, setting up your website, praying past your usual time. It is the everyday victories that make life worth living. Create your achievement Jar or you can just call it your victory Jar.

<u>Spend time with loved ones</u>

There is a difference between being in the same room with someone and deliberately enjoying their presence. Enjoy being with a loved one by intentionally being present when with them.

Call that buddy up and let them know you want to hang out for a good laugh. It is okay to let them know you feel bored with life and just need some shake up. I believe most good friends will love to spend time with you and could help remind you of beautiful moments in your past.

<u>Do something special for you</u>

When was the last time you bought something expensive for yourself? It has always been your spouse, children, parents or siblings on the topmost part of your expenditure list. If you are like me? You could be prioritizing the ministry or business over you. While that may be great, it is important that you and I look after ourselves from time to time.

I encourage you to pick one day in the week when you do something special for yourself. Make that day about you. On that day, write yourself a love note, spend more time than normal affirming your beauty, your skills, your strength and even your flaws. Laugh about the things you didn't do too well. Remind yourself of your human-ness. Enjoy your own company, pamper yourself. Drink that youghurt you've been eyeing, buy and wear that pricey bikini or boxers. Be creative about honouring you; Everything doesn't have to cost money.

God recently gave me this Idea (weekly me day) to help me enjoy life. I chose Mondays as me-day. What day would you pick? Pick a day in which you can really enjoy or soak in the goodness without hurry. If there's no day like that, then create that day either by delegating responsibilities or rescheduling responsibilities. The focus is for you to **thoroughly enjoy** that day without any pressure.

One way to make me-day exciting is to plan your next me-day immediately you are ending the current. Would you go see a movie? Would you get your kids to tell you a story rather than being the story teller? Would you go window shopping? Would you soak in a hot bath longer than usual?

Would you go for a massage? Would you finally do that thing you've wanted to do? Be intentional and creative about your Me-days.

<u>Redress your Job</u>

Sometimes, the kind of job one does can sap off one's excitement in life. Consider changing jobs if you no longer feel fulfilled in one; consider decorating your work station, consider creating a work routine that puts less pressure on you. Avoid letting work pile, don't take more than you can in a day, and vary work day pressure if that's within your control. Use your leave; don't sell it to the company or co-worker. Companies give leave for a reason.

DEALING WITH WANED EXCITEMENT OVER MINISTRY

This happens when you are giving more than you are taking in. We are called to serve/feed others from a place of fellowship with Christ. That's why we feel burned out when we get too busy serving like Martha when we really should be receiving like Mary (Luke 10:38-34).

Take some time out from service. Renew your strength. Passion or excitement will naturally return once you refresh your spirit with the father, your soul with the people who matter to you and your body with the good things of life.

Here are a few reminders to help restore your excitement or passion.

<u>It is okay to cancel</u>
If you are like me, you love to keep your word and show up at an event once you have accepted the invite. However, you must bear in mind that you need to be fit to serve. Therefore, if you find that ministering at some point would be a struggle, it is okay to send a delegate or ask the organizers to get someone to stand in for you. Please inform them well in advance in order not to cause any confusion. Most people don't handle negative surprises well.

<u>It is okay to say No</u>
 It is not wisdom to pack your itinerary full especially when you sense that you are burning out or need some time out. No one is going to kill you if you turned down an invite. God is not going to withdraw his anointing on your life if you didn't accept to speak at that youth conference next week. Space out your Itinerary so you can have time to spend with God and rejuvenate your soul and body in rest.

<u>You are first His sheep before you are the people's shepherd</u>
Sometimes we make the mistake of prioritizing the people we are called to serve above the God who called us to serve. God wants to spend time with you as much as He wants you to minster to others.
Let your shepherd love, care and feed you before you go feed the sheep you shepherd. He is our strength remember? What lasting impact can you actually make if you are not connected with the shepherd, your strength?

<u>You are designed to give from the abundance in your well so don't let it go dry.</u>
When Jesus said abide in me so you can bear fruits, He told us an absolute truth not a subjective one. There's no height you can possibly get to in ministry such that you no longer need to spend time with God anymore in other to minster. Be consistent about your personal time with God. It is that time spent with Him that makes serving in ministry easy.

<u>Rest is part of service</u>
Our mortal bodies would someday give way for immortality. Until then, we have to take care of this earth suit. If you died before your time, you will be doing God a disservice because He is going to need to find someone fit to do the work He already equipped and empowered you to do. Finding replacements is not as easy as we think so let's take care of our bodies so we can live and fulfill our full course according to the plan.

DEALING WITH FEELING STUCKED

Sometimes we lose excitement for life, a relationship, marriage or project because we feel stucked. Being stucked refers to being at a point where things are difficult and stirs negative emotions such as anxiety, frustration, sadness or even anger to the extent that one feels helpless.

While it is part of life to come face to face with really difficult situations which make us question our abilities per time, it is inappropriate to surrender to feelings of hopelessness or helplessness.

HERE IS WHAT TO DO WHEN YOU FEEL STUCKED.

<u>Define the time frame</u>
You may be tempted to condemn yourself and accept the negative voice of reason which tries to make you feel like a failure; do not fall for that scam.

Remind yourself that you are dealing with something in the present, not in the past or in the future. This will help you get a hold on your emotion.

For instance, if you are feeling stucked about not making enough money from your business due to drop in sales? Remind yourself that this drop is happening now and that if you have made even one sale in the past, you can make more sales today and in the future.

When you think this way, the negative voice of reason will not drown your confidence and past successes in oblivion. You will feel and see that you can make it out of your current state.

<u>Break state while it is early</u>
You know that feeling of helplessness, sadness and frustration? It is a state that can mar even the mighty. The moment you notice that you are beginning to feel like that, just break state!

To break state is to do something completely opposite to disrupt the negative feelings. For example, when we are sad, our shoulders drop, our eyes dim, we go quiet, we generally feel heavy and consequently weighed down. To break state, you would need to square your shoulders, shine your eyes to feign excitement, shout or scream to feign joy and jump!

Do it with the intent to feel different and you will. While this doesn't take away the problem that has made you feel stucked, it changes your physiology and puts your brain in an excited state where it is most likely to figure out a solution.

3

PROCRASTINATION

Procrastination makes easy things hard, hard things harder
- Mason Cooley

Toad and Frog

Toad woke up.
"Drat!" he said.
"This house is a mess. I have so much work to do"
Frog looked through the window.
"Toad, you are right," said Frog, "It is a mess."
Toad pulled the covers over his head.
"I will do it tomorrow," said Toad.

"Today I will take life easy."

Frog came into the house.

"Toad," said Frog, "your pants and jacket are lying on the floor."

"Tomorrow," said Toad from under the covers.

"Your kitchen sink is filled with dirty dishes," said Frog.

"Tomorrow," said Toad.

"There is dust on your chairs."

"Tomorrow," said Toad.

"Your windows need scrubbing," said Frog.

"Your plants need watering."

"Tomorrow!" cried Toad.

"I will do it all tomorrow!"

Toad sat on the edge of his bed.

"Blah," said Toad.

"I feel down in the dumps."

"Why?" asked Frog.

"I am thinking about tomorrow," said Toad.

"I am thinking about all of the many things that I will have to do."

"Yes," said Frog, "tomorrow will be a very hard day for you."

"But Frog," said Toad, "If I pick up my pants and jacket right now, then I will not have to pick them up tomorrow, will I?"

"No," said Frog "You will not have to."

Toad picked up his clothes. He put them in the closet.

"Frog," said Toad, "if I wash my dishes right now, then I will not have to wash them tomorrow, will I?"

"No," said Frog. "You will not have to."

Toad washed and dried his dishes. He put them in the cupboard.

"Frog," said Toad, "if I dust my chairs and scrub my windows and water my plants right now, then I will not have to do it tomorrow, will I?"

"No," said Frog. "You will not have to do any of it."

Toad dusted his chairs. He scrubbed his windows. He watered his plants.

"There," said Toad, "Now I feel better. I am not in the dumps anymore."

"Why?" asked Frog.

"Because I have done all that work," said Toad.

"Now I can save tomorrow for something that I really want to do."

"What is that?" asked Frog.

"Tomorrow," said Toad, "I can just take life easy."

Toad went back to bed. He pulled the covers over his head and fell asleep.[1]

** ** **

Procrastination is the action of delaying or postponing something. I love the way Wikipedia says it, " Procrastination is the practice of doing more pleasurable things in place of less pleasurable ones; carrying out less urgent tasks instead of more urgent ones."

It's a good thing you've noticed that you procrastinate. Awareness is the first step to "deliverance".

James Clear's 2-minute rule

I love James Clear's 2-minute rule on dealing with procrastination.
The 2-minute rule is two parts
Part 1: If it takes less than two minutes, then do it now.
The most effective way to stop procrastinating is to act!
See chapter 8 on taking action.
There is no special magic application to killing procrastination other than doing things when they should be done. The next time you are tempted to procrastinate on anything, ask yourself "can I do this under two minutes"? If yes, please get it done immediately.

How about the other parts that takes more than two minutes?

Like Wikipedia states, "Procrastination is the practice of doing more pleasurable things." Start with the task that feels pleasurable. Personally my greatest displeasure on chores is manually doing the laundry.
 I've been writing on halia (my laptop) since 6am. This is 1pm and I'm still enjoying sitting right here and making this book. Meanwhile, I have a heap of clothes due for laundry. Why am I ignoring that to sit here for hours to write? Truth is, I find writing deeply pleasurable.
   Following James' 2-minute rule, I can't get done washing those clothes in 2-minutes. That is so impossible. I also can't get done writing this book today. Therefore, I've applied my

rule of priority to help me do the laundry today.

My rule of priority states,
Begin with the most important task and follow through until the least important tasks are done.

The most important task on my to-do list today is to write six chapters of this book. Therefore, I began with writing. As soon as I reach the target I set for myself, I will go select the number of clothes I can deal with within a time frame (40minutes). Allocating time to an activity you do not enjoy, would help you concentrate and get it over with in time.

Laundry is tiring for me because it takes time. One way I've dealt with the displeasure is to set a time limit to how long I spend doing it. Granted, if I followed the 2-minute rule on this matter, I will have to wash every day. However, that is unrealistic for me; considering I have lots of other higher priority responsibilities beckoning for my attention during the week.

You might be wondering what happens during weekends? Today being a Saturday, is my first stay-home Saturday in the past two months and a few weeks.

So why and how would I end up doing the laundry today? First, I see the need to. Therefore, I will control the laundry duration such that the task ends before it goes from displeasure to being grossly displeasurable.

PROCRASTINATION AND YOUR ASSIGNMENT

Procrastination can be tricky. People let the habit slip into the most important thing in life- Their assignment.

   An assignment is a set of instruction given to you by God concerning the world or/and fellow believers per time.

When you procrastinate about an assignment, you are walking in disobedience. You must remember that you are not in control of sunrise and sunset therefore you must be disciplined enough to do what God assigns to you today.

What has God laid in your heart lately?

What burden is God leading you to lift?

Who is He asking you to help?

It is okay to keep this book and go get it done immediately.

HERE IS HOW TO STOP PROCRASTINATING

Follow the 2-minute rule where applicable:

2-minute rule would work on activities such as washing your plate after a meal, responding to an email as soon as you've read, arranging the files as soon as you remember, reading your notes right after every class, reading a verse of the bible before getting off the bed.

Prioritize:

Distinguish between what's important and what's urgent.

There are four categories anything or situation can be at any given time. These categories are

• Important and Urgent

• Important and not-urgent

• Less important and urgent

• Less important and not-urgent

Using my laundry situation for example: where does my laundry fall? It falls under important and not urgent.
 I have other clothes to wear if I didn't do my laundry this weekend but it is important that I did so the heap in my laundry basket won't grow into an overwhelming size. Where does writing this book fall? It falls under important and urgent because the launch date is a few weeks away. Considering my schedule, I mayn't have the opportunity to commit long hours into writing. Therefore I've got to do this today.
Now use the 4-categories above, to sort your responsibilities out and begin with the most important and urgent ones. Sorting tasks into categories gives you a good start at getting them done.

Be creative:
Look out for ways to make tasks more pleasurable for you.
For me, I've set a time limit to my laundry moments and I sing or hum a favorite song playing on my phone the whole time.
What do you procrastinate about? What needs to happen or be present for you to enjoy or relatively enjoy the task?
Make it happen.

Use the Cartesian questions:
Perhaps you are not procrastinating on an everyday activity.
It could be that you procrastinate on the big things of life such as updating your degree, getting married, starting a business, changing jobs or anything major. Answering the

Cartesian questions can help you find the fuel required to get your engine started. The questions are,

•What WOULD happen if I DID it now?

•What WOULD happen if I DIDN'T do it now?

•What WOULDN'T happen if I DID it now?

• What WOULDN'T happen if I DIDN'T it now?

When we clearly see what might be at stake, we will naturally find the zeal to spring into action.

Celebrate:

Every time you overcome procrastination, throw a little party for yourself. This party could be as little but great as seeing a movie, writing yourself a well-done note, getting cold-stone ice-cream (my favourite treat), basically whatever makes you feel good.

Associating victory with your action will make you want to have more victories over future procrastination temptations.

Like Frog, Procrastination could be a sign of slothfulness/laziness. You can absolutely get rid of laziness. I shared practical tips on dealing with that in my book, 7 Signs you are Sabotaging your Life.

4

DISTRACTION

I rose my eyes in curiosity
Observing the pace of pilgrims
Born with responsibilities
They journey through life

At birth, the blueprint of destiny
Is encoded in their souls
They grow in passion
Sweetly displaying the gifts within

Brilliantly, they align their lives
in a specific direction
With a focused mind
And a heart baptized in zeal
They keep their gaze on their destination

As time rolls by
They grow familiar with their goals
As they say to themselves
" This far have we come
So far we are sure to go
Irrespective of what might be
Hence, let's take a break"

They relax in lethargy
And wallow in the confidence of past glory
While they relapse in achievement
Bathing their journey
in the whirlwind of procrastination

Subtly but firmly
Their attention begins to drift
They now have time
 For things once considered ephemeral
Misplaced priority rules the day
Dexterity repels them
As they settle for less

Distractions are attractive
Cloned in very strong appeal
They demand immediate attention
They come with strong affection
To override ones initial passion
As your appetite for the otiose
Gradually becomes an obsession

Distractions come in various forms and shades
They totally paralyze your quest
Making you worse than an ostrich in wisdom
Nothing kills greatness as fast as this venom called
DISTRACTION[1].

** ** **

Distraction accounts for 90% of road accidents daily. From texting while driving to phone calls, to retouching makeup, to looking too long at something by the corner and more. While road accidents seem like the obvious consequence of distraction, it causes many major accidents in other aspects of life- career, ministry, spiritual life, relationships, marriage and business. Look into your life sincerely, you will agree with me.

As you go about your purpose, you will definitely come face to face with distractions. You have to learn to ignore its seduction in other to escape this storm. The only antidote to distraction is FOCUS.

MASTERING THE ART OF FOCUS

Let's assume that you are staring right ahead of you, anticipating the arrival of the bus scheduled to take you to work; when suddenly you hear a loud bang behind you. Boom!

You turn and it was a bike man who hit a car, leaving about five people injured and a child instantly dead.

Your boss had announced earlier that you were to make a presentation to a client that morning. The presentation if successful, is supposed to get the organization some profit ranging into millions of dollars.

A crowd has gathered at the scene where the accident happened. While you stared and empathized with the casualties of the accident, the bus you were waiting for had gone. The accident apparently wasn't on the lane you were in. You waited to get another bus but this time, the traffic had begun to affect the lane you were in and so It took you a while to find one.

You arrived at the office at past 9am and missed the presentation scheduled for 8:15am.

Was the accident worth your empathy? Yes

Was your presentation important? Yes

Keep this in mind- Focus refers to the **main** or central point of interest or attention.[2]

On your way to work that morning, what was your focus? I presume it would be arriving early at your work place for the presentation. Eventually, the unplanned or unexpected happened and your attention momentarily shifted from catching the bus to the casualties.

If the Boss got you demoted and slashed eighty percent off your pay that month. I guess you would think he is a mean boss right?

You know what honey; Focus doesn't negate the presence of distractions. Therefore learning to focus on the "real thing" in the midst of life's drama is a must have skill to flip your wishes into wins.

Three things I need you to hold on to as we examine mastering the art of focus are **light**, **distractions** and **object.** If you've been to a live stage performance, you will notice that there's a main/prevailing **light** focused on the performer (**object)**, there could be a choir or team of backup singers on stage that spectators don't see but hear.

The "prevailing light" doesn't leave the performer to zoom on the backup singers. Doing such would **distract** the audience from the artist.

Same way, there is a prevailing light cast on people or things every second in time. That prevailing light determines your focus or who/what has your attention.

EVERYONE HAS A FOCUS

Everyone has a focus. We just aren't focusing on the same thing. Therefore the questions to ask are,

- Is my current focus a thing of value?
- How do I control my mind to stay on what is most important?

If you can

- Determine the value/worth of your focus and
- Keep your mind on it in the midst of distraction?

You have gained mastery over the art of FOCUS.

WHAT'S YOUR FOCUS?

The focus of your life reflects your values and how much you are worth at the end of your life.

To determine the focus of your life answer these questions sincerely.

- What do I think on as soon as I awake in the morning?
- Who do I think about first thing in the morning?
- What are my most important (high priority) goals right now?
- What do I consider when making decisions?
- Who do I consider when making decisions?
- Do I readily make sacrifices in other to achieve these goals?
- What am I readily excited about?

These questions would help you determine your focus per time.

WHAT MAKES A FOCUSED PERSON?

1. He/ She has clear goals/**Objectives**
2. He/she has clearly mapped out **strategy** for those goals
3. He/she is **committed** to those goals

In plain English, Focused people **have Objectives, Strategy**

and Commitment.
Do you have those?

THE ART OF FOCUS

I already said Focus isn't the absence of distraction. The most successful people have had to deal with internal and external distractions. The difference between them and those who abandoned their course are these;

Review: Focused people consistently review the object of their attention in light of their clearly stated objectives. When faced with seemingly important things, you must ask "how does this bring me closer to the stated objectives?"
If the answer isn't positive and can't help you achieve the stated goal within the scheduled time? It is a distraction.
 Distractions are often subtle. They could be important too but again, the goal in front of you determines what's more important.

Redress: Focused people redress their commitment regularly. They don't assume that they are committed to their course. They consistently strengthen their commitment towards the set out goals/objectives.
Refer to our opening story.
If you had reviewed your attention (on the scene) you would have realized that your focus was broken. You were in no position to help the victims since you had no car by which to take them to the hospital. You also had a phone with which

to call the paramedic team yet you stood watching while the bus went by.

Everything appears to be worthy of our commitment but there's really one thing that matters per time- Your Objective.

It is your responsibility to redress your commitment to your goals consistently.

THINGS OF WORTH TO FOCUS ON

While you clearly identify your objectives for career, marriage, ministry, relationships, business, engage wisdom and strategically approach your goals consistently (commitment), there are a few things of worth I'll encourage you to focus on.

<u>Things Above:</u>

Since, then, you have been raised with Christ, Set your hearts on things above, Where Christ is seated at the right hand of God. Set your minds on things above, not on earthly things.
Colossians 3:1-2 (NIV)

The key words here are **Seek** and **Set**

Seeking and Setting is the mechanism used when attempting to focus a camera or video lens to best view an image.

To Seek is to intentionally search out God's opinion in matters. To Set is to establish your mind on His opinion. When you do this, you see through the eyes of Christ and become fearless and more productive.

The clause, "focus on things above" doesn't suggest we

should be heaven focused and earthly useless. Rather it says, keep your mind on the real deal (Jesus) from whom you draw sufficient light to make a difference in a dark world (on any sector or platform).

The Right Path:

Proverbs 23:19 says, "Listen my son, and be wise and set your heart on the right path. (NIV)

What is the right path?
Jesus said, "I am the way, the truth and the life"
John 14:6 (NIV)
The right path is neither a system of operation nor an organized thought pattern or mode of operation. The right path is a person – JESUS.

FOCUS ON HIM!

God's Decrees:

The psalmist says *"My heart is set on keeping your decrees to the very end". Psalm 119:112 (NIV)*

Why would he set his heart/focus on God's decrees? It is because *"the law of the Lord is **perfect**, converting the soul and the testimony (decrees) of the Lord is **Sure** (certain) making the simple wise. " Psalm 19:7(NIV)*

The decision to focus on God's decrees is the best you would ever make after the decision to have JESUS in your heart as Lord and Saviour.

I encourage you to

- Focus on things of worth
- Set clear goals
- Map out clear strategy for achieving them.

Commit to your goals in spite of distractions.

Come with me, I will show you how to do these things in part two of this book.

5

ANXIETY

Worry never robs tomorrow of its sorrow, it only saps today of its joy. Leo Buscaglia

Flying in the clouds

A recently licensed pilot was flying his private plane in a cloudy day. He was not very experienced in instrument landing. When the control tower was to bring him in, he began to get panicky. Then a stern voice came over the radio, "You just obey instructions, we'll take care of the obstructions."[1]

Anxiety is a feeling of worry, nervousness, or unease about something with an uncertain outcome. It is a strong desire or concern to do something or for something to happen.[2]

Anxiety is an emotion characterized by an unpleasant state of inner turmoil. It is the subjectively unpleasant feelings of dread over anticipated events.

Anxiety is not the same as fear. While fear is a response to a real or perceived immediate threat, anxiety is the expectation of future threat.[3]

When feelings of anxiety begin to interfere with everyday activities, it is regarded as a mental health issue called anxiety disorder. This storm has rocked many boats and prevented multitude from the wins they deserve.

Based on research at the College of Medicine Ibadan, there are 1.5 million cases of anxiety every year in Nigeria. The research shows that anxiety affects most people within the ages of 6 and above 60, although it is more prevalent in young adults between ages 14 and 60. I find this information disheartening.

Considering this statistics, we can't imagine how many dreams get squashed annually, how many hearts kiss failure before their owners ever try or how many destinies are buried in the cold grip of anxiety. We can't imagine.

TYPES OF ANXIETY DISORDERS

According to National Institute of mental health, there are

five major types of anxiety disorders as seen below;

Generalized Anxiety Disorder (GAD)

An anxiety disorder characterized by chronic anxiety, exaggerated worry and tension, even when there is little or nothing to provoke it.

Obsessive-Compulsive Disorder (OCD)

An anxiety disorder characterized by recurrent, unwanted thoughts (obsessions) and/or repetitive behaviors (compulsions).

Repetitive behaviors such as hand washing, counting, checking, or cleaning are often performed with the hope of preventing obsessive thoughts or making them go away. Performing these so-called "rituals," however, provides only temporary relief, and not performing them markedly increases anxiety.

Panic disorder

An anxiety disorder characterized by unexpected and repeated episodes of intense fear accompanied by physical symptoms that may include chest pain, heart palpitations, shortness of breath, dizziness, or abdominal distress.

Post-Traumatic Stress Disorder (PTSD) is an anxiety disorder that can develop after exposure to a terrifying event or ordeal in which grave physical harm occurred or was threatened. Traumatic events that may trigger PTSD include violent personal assaults such as rape, natural or human-caused disasters, accidents, or military combat.

Social Phobia, or Social Anxiety Disorder

An anxiety disorder characterized by overwhelming anxiety and excessive self-consciousness in everyday social situations. Social phobia can be limited to only one type of situation - such as a fear of speaking in formal or informal situations, or eating or drinking in front of others . In its most severe form, may be so broad that a person experiences symptoms almost anytime they are around other people.

SYMPTOMS OF ANXIETY

The physiological symptoms of anxiety may include[4][5]

<u>Neurological</u>: Headache, Paresthesia, Vertigo, Presyncope
<u>Digestive:</u> Abdominal pain, nausea, diarrhea, indigestion, dry mouth
<u>Respiratory</u>: Shortness of breath, sighing breath
<u>Cardiac</u>: Palpitations, Tachycardia, chest pain Muscular
<u>Cutaneous</u>: Perspiration, Itchy skin
<u>Uro-genital:</u> Frequent Urination, Urinary Urgency, dypareunia, impotence

EFFECTS OF ANXIETY

The effects of anxiety are thus[6];

<u>Behavioral effects</u>**:**

This includes withdrawal from situations which have

provoked anxiety or negative feelings in the past, changes in sleeping patterns, changes in habits, increase or decrease in food intake, restlessness and increased motor tension such as foot tapping, cloth twisting, hand wringing (excessive display of concern or distress).

Emotional effects:
This includes feelings of apprehension or dread, trouble concentrating, feeling tense or jumpy, anticipating the worst, irritability, restlessness, watching (and waiting) for signs (and occurrences) of danger, and feeling like your mind's gone blank as well as nightmares/bad dreams, obsessions about sensations, déjà vu, a trapped-in-your-mind feeling, and feeling like everything is scary.

Cognitive effects:
This include thoughts about suspected dangers, such as fear of dying. You may fear that the chest pains are a deadly heart attack or that the shooting pains in your head are the result of a tumor or an aneurysm. An intense fear when you think of dying, or you may think of it more often than normal, or can't get it out of your mind.

CAUSES OF ANXIETY

What causes anxiety and anxiety disorders can be complicated. It's likely that a combination of factors, including genetics and environmental reasons, play a role. However, it's clear that some events, emotions, or experiences may cause symptoms of anxiety to begin or may make them worse. These events, emotions or experiences are called triggers[7].

Most people find they have multiple triggers. But for some people, anxiety attacks can be triggered for no reason at all. Identifying your triggers is an important step in managing them[7].

Anxiety triggers can be different for each person, but many triggers are common among people with these conditions.

<u>Health Issues:</u> People get anxious when they get sad news about their health or the health of a loved one. The news evokes personal feelings that trigger anxiety.

<u>Medications:</u> Active ingredients in birth control pills, cough and congestion medication and weight loss drugs may contain active ingredients that make you feel uneasy or unwell. It is advisable that you stop taking such and meet your doctor for a new prescription once you notice anxiety symptoms as a result.

<u>Caffeine:</u> I don't think Nigerians consume a lot of caffeine. For those who do, a study in 2010 shows that caffeine triggers or worsens anxiety. Reduce your intake as much as possible. You should also look for better alternatives.

<u>Skipping Meals:</u> It is known fact that food can affect people's mood. It definitely affects mine (Laughs). When you don't

eat, your blood sugar may drop. That can lead to jittery hands and a rumbling tummy. It can also trigger anxiety. So long as you are not fasting, please eat. Don't let work or anything make you go long hours without food. Studies show that healthy snacks (if you can't get a meal at the time) are a great way to prevent low blood sugar, feelings of nervousness, agitation and anxiety.

Negative thinking: Your mind controls much of your body. When you're upset or frustrated, the words you say to yourself can trigger feelings of anxiety. If you use negative words when thinking about yourself, learning to refocus your language and feelings to positive, when you catch yourself thinking negatively about you will help.

Financial concerns: Unexpected bills, due bills, debts can trigger anxiety.

Parties or social events: Do you hate been in a room full of strangers? You are not alone. Events that require you to make small talk or interact with people you don't know can trigger feelings of anxiety, which may be diagnosed as social anxiety disorder.

Personal triggers: These triggers may be difficult to identify, but a mental health specialist is trained to help people identify them. These may begin with a smell, a place, or even a song. Personal triggers remind you, either consciously or unconsciously, of a bad memory or traumatic event in your life. Individuals with post-traumatic stress disorder (PTSD) frequently experience anxiety from environmental triggers.

Identifying personal triggers may take time, but it's important so you can learn to overcome them.

<u>Examination/Interviews:</u> I have a dear student who almost literally couldn't breathe days leading to her exams. She cries profusely and thinks negatively. She feels unprepared no matter how hard she has studied. It may surprise you to know that this girl is one of the school's brightest student. Yet every time examination is approaching, the days leading to the exam becomes a turmoil. Does examination trigger anxiety in you?

<u>Public events or performances:</u> I remember trembling before a congregation in church when I was 5 years old. I was supposed to recite a memory verse but forgot my lines and started to cry. Thank God for my mum who didn't let that be my last time on stage. She prepared me the next Sunday and sent me back in front of over 200 adults. I didn't want to do it anymore but she insisted. She told me to look above their heads. I did as she said and managed to get my lines correctly. The recitation was Psalms 122:1-2(KJB).

"I will lift up mine eyes unto the hills,
from whence cometh my help.
My help cometh from the LORD,
which made heaven and earth.

I can never forget those verses. I stood trembling as the

congregation gave me a standing ovation. Although happy that I did good, I still cried.

Anxiety can mess one up. There I was crying and shaking in my moment of victory. Thank God for my mum. Years after, I am touring the world as a public speaker. I don't deny that I still feel signs of anxiety such as tummy butterflies, shaky hands and trembling feet when I stand before my audience but I have learnt to deal with that.

I will show you how to handle anxiety as you read on and I dedicated a good deal of time and pages in helping you deal with specific anxiety issues in **turn wishes to wins workbook**. You will find extensive activities and detailed help in there.

<u>Stress:</u> Daily pressures caused by traffic jam and the hustle and bustle of city life can trigger anxiety.

<u>Conflict:</u> Having peace in your marriage or relationship is very vital for your mental health. Conflicts at your workplace, religious or social group can trigger anxiety.

HOW TO HANDLE ANXIETY

The unprecedented conversation turns on in your head;
What if I fail?
What if it doesn't work out?
What if I get disappointed?
What if they change their mind?
What if they don't love or accept me?

What if they …
What if it...
What if I...
What if she....
What if he...
What if we....
Then our hearts begin to pound faster than usual, belly tightens up, palms sweat profusely, sadness and gloom cloud our hearts as though the "what if" already happened.

I have had several what if moments. Many happened, others didn't.
However, I have learnt that getting a what-if conversation going on in my head is not as important as what I do with it. Losing our peace and joy after a what-if conversation isn't God's will for us. It definitely isn't want you want either.

Anxiety grips your heart when you envisage that an event in the future might turn out in an unpleasant way. Since we can't often completely control what happens in the future, how do we handle the waiting period between the what-if and the actual occurrence (or not) of our expectations?

<u>Track it:</u>
I've had several experiences when a 'what If' was my mind's way of prepping me before the arrival of a shocking news or event. I learnt to track my thoughts and treat them as an opportunity to prepare for the unwanted.
So rather, than sweat in anxiety, take the mental suggestion as an expo on how to respond should it happen.

<u>Face it:</u>

I know how we often want to say, "God forbid" that can't be me. Yeah, it can't be you but it definitely would be someone. So what if it is you? That's the question your mind is trying to ask. Therefore, sweeping it underneath the carpet isn't the best thing to do. Acknowledge the fear, concern or root of worry and admit that you feel whatever emotion is in there.

<u>Release it:</u>

 As a model for release, some people pray, some people journal, others talk to people about it. I do all three and more. Just do what works for you.

One effective way to release anxiety is to talk to God about it. The Philippians 4:6-7 model is such a perfect expeller of anxiety when applied in faith. It says,

*"Be anxious for nothing, but in everything by **prayer** and **supplication,** with **thanksgiving,** let your requests be made known to God. And the peace of God, which surpasses all understanding, will guard your hearts and your minds in Christ Jesus. (ESV)"*

I see Philippians 4:6-7 as a command rather than an advice.
A command to **turn anxiety into answered prayers.**
So a 'what if' hits your head/heart rather than let anxiety ruin the moments of Joy in your life, what do you do?
Pray: Express your wishes
Supplicate: State you specific heartfelt need/desire/expected outcome to God.
Give thanks: Thank Him for the outcome (all things works

for your good remember?) regardless of how it plays out in the end.

And receive the reward of peace that is way beyond your view would encapsulate your mind and heart.

So the next time anxiety knocks on the door, **track it, face it** and **release it** using the Philippians 4:6 model.

I understand that praying alone doesn't work for some people. Here are some effective psychological treatments that I find really helpful when I work with clients dealing with Anxiety.

Spaghetti body Exercise

This exercise is inspired by the wiggly nature of wet or cooked Spaghetti. When you are anxious or nervous, your body feels tight. The goal of this exercise is to help your body feel lighter and free. This in turn influences your mind to relax and purges you free of anxiety.

I suggest you read the instruction below aloud and record as you read. You will follow your recorded instruction when it is time to practice. It will be more effective than if you were to read and practice simultaneously. The recorded audio will also serve as a handy instructor for times when anxiety tries to creep back in your heart.

Let's go

1. Scrunch your hands very tight. You can even grunt if that helps. Now, spaghetti your hands very loose. Great job!

2. If you were sitted before, now stand up. Scrunch your belly very tight. Count 1-3. Then make it Spaghetti loose.
3. Scrunch your feet. 1,2,3. Now Spaghetti!
4. Scrunch your legs. 1,2,3. Now Spaghetti!
5. Scrunch your bottom! 1,2,3. Now Spaghetti. (Repeat for shoulders, arms, hands, neck, face, eyes).
6. Great job! You did Spaghetti Body! You should feel pretty loose and wiggly all over.

Gauging your stress level

Earlier, I mentioned that stress causes anxiety. Take this quiz below to determine your current level of stress.

For each of the following experiences, indicate to what degree it has been a part of your life over the past month by writing in the appropriate number.

1 = not at all part of my life

2 = only slightly part of my life

3 = distinctly part of my life

4 = very much part of my life

Let's go

____ 1. Disliking your daily activities

____ 2. Lack of privacy

____ 3. Disliking your work

____ 4. Ethnic or racial conflict

____ 5. Conflicts with in-laws or boyfriend's/girlfriend's family

____ 6. Being let down or disappointed by friends

____ 7. Conflict with supervisor(s) at work

____ 8. Social rejection

___ 9. Too many things to do at once

___ 10. Being taken for granted

___ 11. Financial conflicts with family members

___ 12. Having your trust betrayed by a friend

___ 13. Separation from people you care about

___ 14. Having your contributions overlooked

___15. Struggling to meet your own standards of performance and accomplishment

___ 16. Being taken advantage of

___ 17. Not enough leisure time

___ 18. Financial conflicts with friends or fellow workers

___ 19. Struggling to meet other people's standards of performance and accomplishment

___ 20. Having your actions misunderstood by others

___ 21. Cash-flow difficulties

___ 22. A lot of responsibilities

___ 23. Dissatisfaction with work

___ 24. Decisions about intimate relationship(s)

___ 25. Not enough time to meet your obligations

___ 26. Dissatisfaction with your mathematical ability

___ 27. Financial burdens

___28. Lower evaluation of your work than you think you deserve

___ 29. Experiencing high levels of noise

___30. Adjustments to living with unrelated person(s) (e.g., roommate)

___ 31. Lower evaluation of your work than you hoped for

___ 32. Conflicts with family member(s)

___ 33. Finding your work too demanding

____ 34. Conflicts with friend(s)

____ 35. Hard effort to get ahead

____ 36. Trying to secure loan(s)

____37. Getting "ripped off" or cheated in the purchase of goods

____ 38. Dissatisfaction with your ability at written expression

____ 39. Unwanted interruptions of your work

____ 40. Social isolation

____ 41. Being ignored

____ 42. Dissatisfaction with your physical appearance

____ 43. Unsatisfactory housing conditions

____ 44. Finding work uninteresting

____ 45. Failing to get money you expected

____ 46. Gossip about someone you care about

____ 47. Dissatisfaction with your physical fitness

____ 48. Gossip about yourself

____49.Difficulty dealing with modern technology (e.g., computers)

____ 50. Car problems

____ 51. Hard work to look after and maintain home

____ Total

Now, add up your responses and find your total and corresponding stress level below.

≥ 136 Very high stress

116–135 High stress

76–115 Average stress

56–75 Low stress

51–55 Very low stress

There are many effective ways to deal with stress. Below is my personal go to guy when I am stressed and NEED to keep working on a task.

Deep Breathing Exercise
Again, you read the instruction aloud and record your voice for use when you need it.
Let's go,

Make the air come in through your nose and out of your mouth.
Now, make sure you are sitting up straight. Make sure your feet are down. This makes the air better for you.
Take a long, slow tunnel of air into your nose.
Take a long, slow tunnel of air out of your mouth.
Remember to breathe in and out, slow and long.
(Sometimes, moving your hands with the air can help.)
Great job!

You can use deep Breathing technique when you feel stressed, in the middle of traffic, just before you walk up a stage to speak to an audience, when you stand in front of an interview panel or sit in from of your examination paper. I personally love Deep Breathing exercise because it is like a super-secret skill that you can use right in front of people and they might never notice!

Remember to get **turn wishes to wins workbook**. I dedicated a good deal of time, expertise and pages in helping you deal with the storms of fear, waned excitement, procrastination, distraction and anxiety. Now you have no excuse not to turn your wishes into wins!

EXECUTE MISSIONS

EXECUTE MISSIONS

Execute every act of thy life as though it were thy last.
  Marcus Aurelius

When the gate drops, it's time to try and execute the best you can. **Nate Holland**

If you don't execute your ideas, they die.
  Roger Von Oech

The proof is in the results, and the proof will be in the ongoing ability to execute.
Mindy Grossman

The hand can never execute anything higher than the heart can imagine. **Ralph Waldo Emerson**

The greatest training in the world is absolutely worthless without the will to execute it properly, consistently and with intensity. **John Romaniello**

The method of the enterprising is to plan with audacity and execute with vigor **Christian Nestell Bovee**

I sometimes think less is more. If you cut yourself in too many places, It is hard to execute.
Philip Green

Either I will find a way or I will make one.
Philip Sydney

Start where you are; Use what you have; Do what you can.
Arthur Ashe

The most effective way to do it is to do it.
Amelia Earhart

6

THE POWER OF DESIRE

The size of your success is measured by the strength of your desire- Robert Kiyosaki (American Author and Successful businessman).

I believe one of the beautiful gifts of the human soul is the ability to desire. A desire is a strong feeling of wanting to have something or wishing for something to happen[1].

The reason most people doubt the capacity of their desires to manifest is because they have many other unfulfilled desires. The challenge with unfulfilled desires is not that desire in itself lack the potential or capacity to manifest. The challenge most times is that we don't even know for sure what we desire.

DO YOU KNOW WHAT YOU REALLY DESIRE?

Perhaps, you think you desire wealth. You have told yourself that you will be happier if you had more money in the bank. While that sounds like a legit desire, what you actually desire might be more control over your time so you can tour the world on vacation, being able to provide anything at any time for your family, being able to live in the choicest part of the earth, being able to wear designer brands without sweating over the cost. It is important that your desires are clear so you can feel deeply fulfilled and satisfied when they eventually manifest.

The reason most people feel dissatisfied after achieving a goal they fought so hard and long to grasp is also because they thought that was what they really desired. For instance, A lady could spend all her time strongly chasing marriage only to eventually get married and realize she just wanted financial security not the weight and wins of a marriage.

Deep feelings of fulfillment and satisfaction are tied to the clarity of your desire.

If you sense you desire a house? Ask yourself, "Why do I want a house?" Could it be that I want to feel significant in my home town? If so, are there other ways I could achieve this feeling of significance other than building or buying a house? Could it be that I want an added stream of income? If so, is buying or building a house, the best way to fulfill this desire? When you question your desires, you uncover the real thing you desire. Questioning your desires births clarity. Clarity in turn saves you from wasting energy, time and resources chasing after a desire and dream you wouldn't be happy with in the end.

When you know exactly what you desire, your subconscious mind (the part of your consciousness that your brain isn't focusing on) begins to recognize and attract opportunities for your desires to manifest.

HOW TO CLARIFY YOUR DESIRES

Below are five practices I apply in clarifying my desires. You can apply them on any desire your heart conceives.

<u>Scrutinize intentions:</u>
To scrutinize is to examine or inspect closely and thoroughly. When a desire wells up in your heart, find out its aim by asking," why do I have this desire?"

Intentions births or creates our reality. Finding out why you suddenly desire something is an effective way to recognize what's healthy or unhealthy for your spirit, soul and body. Healthy desires spur you to succeed in your purpose, godliness and life generally. An unhealthy desire detracts you from succeeding in your purpose, godliness and life. You want to make sure that the desires you house and manifest are the ones that better you and the world around you.

For instance, if you noticed a sudden desire to be wealthy? Scrutinizing the intention of that desire would involve genuinely answering questions like,

Do I want wealth just because someone else has it?

Do I want wealth because I want to prove a point to my ex who doesn't care less about me or my dog?

Do I want it because it will help me fulfill a higher purpose? What higher purpose would being wealthy help me fulfill?

An example of a higher purpose could be to fund the education of less privileged students in your village, to sponsor conferences that educate and promote productivity in young people, To help war torn nations recover.

Don't try to impose a higher purpose that isn't present just because you want to justify your desire. The key word in this practice is honesty. You may choose to deceive others (I plead that you don't though), but you **must not** deceive yourself.

Explore Emotions:

An emotion is any conscious experience characterized by intense mental activity and certain degree of pleasure or displeasure.[1]

What sort of emotions does this desire evoke within you? Does it evoke fear, anger, sadness or grief, shame, joy, disgust, surprise, trust, anticipation, envy, love, pity, jealousy, confidence or hatred?

Exploring your emotions require that you answer the following questions sincerely;

what do I feel?

Why do I feel what I feel?

Is this a feeling or emotion I want to retain in my life?

If you feel joy? Ask, why do I feel joyful about my desire?

If you feel shame? Ask, Why am I ashamed of this desire? As you do this, you will begin to see clearly into the atmosphere that desire will create in your life should it eventually manifest. You will then be able to decide if that's the kind of atmosphere you want to live your life in.

Word-Match :

I believe the bible is the infallible word of God and therefore is fit to judge my desires. When I notice a desire lurking in the crevice of my soul, I search for a scripture that addresses the desire. I have found that there is absolutely nothing that the bible does not directly or indirectly address.

Matching your desires against God's word helps keep you in check. You don't want to house, nurse and manifest ungodly desires like murder, greed or anything that influences you to mess with the occult.

Value-check :

Weigh the desire against your values. Is the desire consistent with your values? Perhaps, you value happiness and suddenly notice a desire to marry a man or woman who is quarrelsome just because they are good looking and rich. Your desire obviously doesn't match with your value of happiness. Do you really want to marry such a person or you are just attracted to their good looks and paycheck?

Value-checking your desire would not only help you clarify what you really desire. It will also ensure that your heart retains and manifests only those desires that align with your values.

<u>Pen-test:</u>

Pen-testing is my description of writing down your desires. There is some connection I am yet to unravel about the mind, pen and paper. When you write down your desires, you will able to decide if it is really what you want.

A written desire gives form to the faint vapor lurking in your mind. You will be able to see it in 3-D and decide if that's what you really want.

Assuming someone (not you) desires to see her sister trip, fall and break a leg, because her sister hurt her terribly the previous day. A written desire would be, *I want my sister to fall and break her leg*. When you read that written desire, you will notice an agitation stirring in your heart. Emotions of shame and guilt may begin to well up in your heart. You will then be able to decide if such a desire is something you should house. Basically, writing down your desires help you see their true weights and colour.

WHAT IS THE STRENGTH OF YOUR DESIRE?

You've been wishing you could be this or that; have that or those; go here or there; but have you spent time to examine the intensity of your desire? How badly do you want God's promises over your life to play out? How badly do you want to see that business thrive? How badly do you want to go from being obese, sick and tired to being the right weight, healthy and strong? How badly do you want your marriage to work? How badly do you want those wishes to leave vapour realm and manifest visibly? How badly?

Just like clarity, the intensity of your desire is pivotal to its manifestation.

Even God regards clear and intense desire. In Genesis 11, we see a people with a clear and intense desire to build a tower high enough to get them to God's abode.

"And the LORD said, Behold, the people is one, and they have all one language; and this they begin to do: and now nothing will be restrained from them, which they have imagined to do." Genesis 11:6 (KJB)

They were going to succeed. Nothing was going to stop them because they were united. We often point out unity as the main reason God said nothing could stop them; but if we looked closely, we would see that unity was a by-product of a clear and intense desire. One man caught the idea and because they all spoke the same language, he effectively communicated his idea to the others. This made them all have a clear desire which they strongly wanted to accomplish.

I ask again, how badly do you want it?

HOW TO INTENSIFY YOUR DESIRE

The human body has five major senses. The senses of sight, smell, taste, feeling, and hearing. These five senses are the pathways by which information travels into the mind.

A weak desire or a strong desire for anything is dependent on how much of that thing we take in through any of these five senses. Therefore if you want to intensify your desire for something, go have a taste, go look at it, go feel it, go listen to it, go perceive it.

Do you desire a certain car but can't afford it yet? Don't worry, go test drive it. The experience will flood your heart with a strong desire to own it. Do you desire a house by the ocean? Go on vacation and stay in one. If you can't afford it? Simply cut off a picture of a house like the type you desire and paste where you can see it often. The sight of the picture house, will intensify your desire to own the real thing. This is the psychology or science behind vision boards.

Do you desire to walk in a certain dimension of God's grace and power as a minister? Get videos of those who already operate in that dimension and your desire for that realm will burn intensely.

If there is any desire you don't want to fuel? Protect your pathways from feeding your mind with information related to it. For instance, if you don't want to fornicate, don't listen to sex-toned songs, don't see sex-toned movies, don't let him/her touch you in an arousing way.

Desire is basically written in garbage in garbage out codes.

HOW DESIRES INFLUENCE YOUR RESULTS

Most people set goals for themselves that they never grasp because they lack a **clear**, **strong** desire for it.

Karim Hajee (an Award Winning Television Reporter in Canada and the United States) on his blog creating power, references famous people with notable achievement in his attempt to explain how desires are critical to our success. He says,

After he lost his most recent fight Mike Tyson said: "I lost my desire, I'm not hungry anymore. I'm wealthy, my kids have money, I have nothing to fight for."

Tyson's desire to fight was to be wealthy and make sure that his family was financially secure. Filling his ego with the notion that he was heavyweight champ didn't matter anymore. Since he had the money – fighting wasn't necessary to him and there was no desire to fight. He wanted to make some more money, he wanted to come back and be champ again - but he had no real desire.

Muhammad Ali, on the other hand, had a burning desire to be heavyweight champion of the world.

His desire wasn't money - it was fame. That's why he always came back - until his body could no longer fulfill his desire.

Nelson Mandela had a burning desire not just for personal freedom - but for the freedom of all blacks in South Africa.

Bill Gates has a desire to see a computer in every home in the world – and we're almost at that point.

Warren Buffet has a desire to make money by investing - and he continues to be successful.

Think about a time in your life when you bagged a notable achievement, you will notice that it wasn't by accident. You had a clear desire for it.

I urge you to be intentional about your desires because they influence your results.

HOW TO MANIFEST YOUR DESIRES

A desire has manifested when it moves from living in your heart or the dream world to being your reality in real life.

Humans are powerful beings and have the capacity to reproduce desires just as God did in Genesis when he desired and called forth light out of darkness.

Everything God created, he first desired. Being made in his likeness, we have the capacity to manifest our desires.

While the rest of this book shows you applicable principles that you can wield to turn your wishes into wins and desires into achievements, I will like to quickly show you a few things about manifesting your desires at this point.

Manifesting your desires hinges on what I call **the**

governing forces of manifestation. These forces are

The law of **belief**,

The law of **utterance**

The law of **request**,

The law of **forgiveness**,

The law of **visualization** and

The law of **attraction**.

In mark 11, Jesus and his disciples were strolling past a fig tree at a time when Jesus was hungry. He looked at the fig tree expecting to find fruits when it was clearly not its season. Disappointed, Jesus said no one was ever going to eat of the tree. The next morning, as they passed by the fig tree, the disciples noticed that the tree had withered from the roots to the tips of all the leaves. This occurrence shocked the disciples. Peter remembered that Jesus had cursed the tree the previous day and he called Jesus' attention to the tree. Being the ever ready teacher that Jesus was, he seized the opportunity to unravel the governing forces of manifestation to his disciples in the verses below.

Then Jesus said to the disciples, "Have faith in God. I tell you the truth, you can say to this mountain, 'May you be lifted up and thrown into the sea,' and it will happen. But you must really believe it will happen and have no doubt in your heart. I tell you, you can pray for anything, and if you believe that you've received it, it will be yours. But when you are praying, first forgive anyone you are holding a grudge against, so that your Father in heaven will forgive your sins, too."
Mark 11:22-25 (NLT)

From the above scripture, we see;

The Law of belief: Whatever you believe and feel becomes your reality.

The Law of utterance: Whatever you say becomes your reality.

The Law of request: You get what you ask for.

The Law of forgiveness: When you release offenders, you release yourself to receive.

The Law of visualization: What you imagine becomes your reality.

The Law of attraction: You attract what you think, believe, say and focus on.

These laws are universal and deliver to anyone regardless of colour, skin, gender, financial or salvation status. It was by these laws that God manifested his desire at creation as recorded in the book of Genesis. You manifest your desires by engaging the forces of manifestation. Here is how to do so

Clarify your desire:
 I taught you how to do that earlier. Once you are sure of what you want, you should

Forgive offenders:
Bearing grudges and housing offences drains your inner strength. When we are hurt, we both consciously and

subconsciously rehearse the pain in our heart. We want the person to be punished. We want good to be withheld from them because of what they did to us.

Jesus says, before you ask for anything, first forgive your offenders. The apparent reason Jesus stated forgiving offenders is so that we can be forgiven also; but when we look underneath those words, I believe Jesus was also saying we should release our offenders so we can be free. Free to receive the good we desire, deserve and seek. When you hold an offender hostage, you are saying it is okay for God to regard your offences and permit the universe to deny you the manifestation of your desire.

One question I will like you to answer is "what is more important to me? Actualizing my dreams or holding my offender?" If you have decided that your dreams are of higher importance to you, then forgive your offender and go ahead to

<u>Ask for what you desire:</u>

Ask for what you want in prayer. Some people, who engage these governing forces of manifestation, pray to the universe. Personally, I pray to God the father through Jesus Christ His son and in the name of that son, Jesus. I do not believe in praying to the universe, because the universe is a creature and as such is inferior to God. The universe is only responding to these laws because God made it to; not because the universe is powerful in itself.

If you noticed, the first words Jesus said in our scriptural text above was "Have faith in GOD!" Jesus didn't say have faith in the universe or 'mother earth', have faith in your own wisdom, knowledge, eloquence or mortality. He said, have faith in God.

The Greek words used for have and faith in that verse are echó[2] which means to possess and pistis[3] derived from the Greek word *peithô*, which means to be persuaded.

Therefore when Jesus said have faith in God He was saying, possess/hold a persuasion/conviction that is rooted in the identity and ability of God. This means that the possibility that you will receive your request is not dependant on your qualification, connection or gender. It is dependent on the identity of God as sovereign and His ability to bend impossibilities for those who put their trust in Him. It was this truth Jesus called our attention to when he said, "WITH GOD ALL THINGS ARE POSSIBLE." Mathew 19:26. The other person Jesus declared that all things are possible with, is the person who believes (Mark 9:23). That is why you must

Purge your belief:

Belief is an acceptance that something is true especially one without proof. To manifest your desire, you must accept your desire as true even if you see no proof yet.

Get rid of any atom of doubt. One way to effectively get rid of doubts is to question your doubts.

When the what-if -it -doesn't -happen -bees buzz in your head, buzz right back with what if it happens?

Then, focus on the positive thought that says it will happen. Next,

<u>Visualize your desire:</u>

To visualize is to form a mental image of something incapable of being viewed or not visible at that moment. Most people practice visualization without knowing that they are using a powerful ability of the mind.

Practice consciously imagining your desires come to pass. For instance, If you desire an award at school or the office, spend time imagining that you have been called up the stage in front of school mates, colleagues, friends and family to receive the award.

Imagine hearing the hands clapping loudly and voices screaming your name. Imagine that they all arise as you walk up the stage and the lights flash brightly over you indicating that you are the one in the spotlight. As you see this, you will begin to feel happy as though it were happening for real and yes it is real even though it is not in the physical realm yet.

Being humans, we are spirits who live in bodies. Whatever you experience in your mind or soul realm is as real as the physical realm. It is only a matter of time before experiences translate from the soul/mind realm into the physical. Be careful what you imagine. If you don't want something to happen, to dwell on the imagination.

<u>Affirm your desires:</u>

Affirmation involves making declarations, confessions, pronouncements, or utterances concerning what you desire.

Christians and non-Christians alike practice affirmations and it works. You only need to believe in your utterance.

I suggest you write out a list of daily affirmations that you declare aloud. It is okay if at first you don't believe what you are saying but don't shut your mouth. Keep saying it. Eventually your mind would believe what your mouth has uttered. Remember Romans 10:17? It says *"Faith comes by hearing especially when it is God's word"* (Paraphrased).

I don't know why, but the human mind believes what it hears often.

<u>Stay thankfully expectant</u>:

When you are expecting something to happen? Your subconscious mind focuses on helping you indentify suitable opportunities for the desire to manifest.

Practice being thankful. Thank God for both the big and small things. Don't just thank Him for granting your desires; thank Him for exceeding your expectations. Thank Him for others who already have what you desire. Genuinely celebrate those who have what you desire.

USE THESE TECHNIQUES TO WORK OUT THE ASSIGNMENTS GOD HAS PLACED IN YOUR HEART.

- Believe what He said you will become
- Focus on what He intends to do in, through, with and for you
- Declare/affirm what He said you will become
- Visualize what He said and

- Hold no grudge against anyone who doesn't help or who attacks you.

7

THE POWER OF DECISION

There is no wrong time to make the right decision- Dalton McGuinty (Canadian Politician)

A decision is a conclusion or resolution reached after considering several possibilities (options). It is a beautiful thing that you desire to be someone better, to be used by God, to make impart, to build a business, to eat healthily, to lose weight, to save some money, to get married, to have children, to go to the university and all that. Sadly, desire without decision is a wishy-washy wish.

Decision gives power and specification to your desires. If you don't decide to become someone or get something, your desires will never see the break of dawn.

God desired a companion that looked and acted like Him he decided to call that companion man and clearly expressed his decision when He said, *"Let us make man in our image, in our likeness, and let them rule over..."* Genesis 1:26.

Every word in that verse was decisive. We see God's desire being specified as a man in His image, likeness and with the power to rule.

The power to make decisions is unique to God and man and is enshrined in a capacity called WILL. In exception of fallen angels who rebel against God, angels don't make their own decisions. They follow God's order.

Animals don't make decisions they simply respond to their immediate environment. Your dog or fowl won't go to a grocery store, and decide to pick an item because it read through the nutritional facts. If it picked anything, it's simply because it thinks it should eat it. The ability to think is not the same as the ability to make decisions. Decision making is a more complex process than capturing thoughts.

Making a decision over a meal involves several considerations such as your nutritional needs, the taste of the food, the length of time it will take to prepare it, whether or not you know how to prepare it, the cost of the food and possibly the number of people who will join in the meal.

Animals don't have the capacity to process information on

that level. While you can desire and decide to eat a meal not readily available in your country, animals can only eat what's in their immediate environment.

For instance, you might want one of those sumptuous Chinese meals. You can decide to drive down to one of their restaurant and order the exact meal you desire. Animals can't wake up on a Monday and decide to eat the other animal that ran by last week. They simply respond to situations as they come.

Get the point?

Being decisive about your desires is so important because when you make a decision, your subconscious awaken to possibilities you couldn't see earlier.

The power to decide is one of the greatest abilities of man. How you wield it determines what becomes of your life and purpose.

HOW TO HARNESS THE POWER OF DECISION

To harness is to control something in other to use it effectively (Cambridge dictionary). Today is a product of yesterday's decision; the future is a product of today's decision. If decisions are powerful enough to alter the directions of our lives, then we must learn to control and wield it for our utmost benefit.

Here is how to harness the power of decision.

<u>Identify the target:</u>

What are you aiming at? What problem do you intend to solve? What need do you want to meet? What goal do you want to achieve? What desire do you want to manifest? Know exactly what you want before you make decisions. You achieve this by quizzing yourself. Answer the questions, what do I want, how do I want it, when and where do I want it?

<u>Scale your options:</u>

Options are a set of possibilities that you choose from. I noticed that I feel overwhelmed when I have to choose from a lot of options. Hence, I try to scale my options often.

Scaling options require that you reduce your options (by eliminating the less relevant) to the most important or necessary, and then make a decision based on the few best options.

For instance, Assuming you intend to school in Nigeria, when applying for the university, don't analyze over one hundred higher institutions found in the Joint Admissions Matriculation Board (JAMB) brochure. It will drain you, make you overwhelmed and you most likely would end up making a poor decision. **Scale your options using what I call uncompromisable factors.**

Uncompromisable factors are those set of conditions that you cannot give up. They include values, faith, special clauses over your health, standards and relationships.

Assuming one is battling with asthma or pneumonia, you will already be setting yourself up for poor decision if you included schools located in extremely cold regions amongst your options. Your health is apparently an uncompromisable factor at this point. Simply eliminate those schools located in zones with extreme temperature.

At the restaurant, I hate to look through a Menu. While I love the power of freedom that variety offers, I also hate to be confused. Therefore, I don't spend time analyzing the menu. I simply look for the familiar and order it. Even though I would love to try something new, I do not want to spend valuable time and energy weighing my options-deciding on which is of a higher nutritional value, which is good value for money, which one wouldn't make me nauseous and all that. If someone (whose decision I trust) decided for me, I will gladly eat what they pick.

While many options arm you with power, too many options lead to waste of time, energy and even confusion. The fewer your options, the better your chance at making a quality decision.

Successful people like the late Steve jobs, Mark Zuckerberg and former President Barack Obama understand and harness the power of decisions by scaling options too.

Steve Jobs was known for wearing a black turtle neck shirt, a pair of jeans and sneakers to work. He probably had like 15 of those black turtle neck shirts. Barack Obama only wears black or navy blue colour suit. Mark Zuckerberg wears a gray T-shirt all the time.

It's not because these men don't like other colors. They just want to eliminate options when it comes to dressing up each morning. This saves them the energy required to make effective decisions in other areas that are most important to them. They also considered <u>uncompromisable factors</u> such as

 <u>Comfort</u>: Why would anyone wear a sneakers if they aren't looking to be comfortable?

<u>Official colours</u>: Steve wore black, Obama wears black or blue, Mark wears gray.

<u>Personal preference</u>: Steve wore a turtle neck shirt, Obama wears suits, Mark wears a T-shirt.

While you may find wearing the same thing to work boring (if you are like me), you really should look out for other areas in your life where you need to scale options by elimination. Does deciding on what to cook give you headache or make you go late to work? Use a meal schedule to plan the family's meal.

 I personally hate to think about what to eat. It drains me. A meal schedule saves time because you just wake up knowing exactly what you are going to prepare.

 Prepare work clothes during the weekend. Choose what to wear on each day of the week. Get them ready, wake up, wear them and go slay. People (especially females) go late for events because we spend a lot of time trying to decide what to wear.

<u>Choose:</u>

The power to choose is cousin to the power to decide. You can't claim to have made a quality decision if you have not chosen from a set of options. If you decide not to choose, you still made a decision. The decision to not choose from a set of options has its benefits and consequences as much as when you decide to choose from a set of options.

When you decisively choose, you leverage the power of your will into manifesting a desirable or undesirable outcome. You therefore must critically weigh the benefits and consequences of your options before choosing. One tool to help you explore and the consequences or outcomes of your options is the Cartesian set of questions. They are to be asked in the order presented below.

What **will** happen if I **do** or choose A? (Write down all the possible outcomes or your action or choice)

What **won't** happen if I **did** or chose A? (Write down all the possible outcomes or your action or choice)

What **will** happen if I **don't do** or choose A? (Write down all the possible outcomes or your action or choice)

What **won't** happen if I **don't do** or choose A? (Write down all the possible outcomes or your action or choice)

For instance,

If you are about to decide whether or not to quit your job to build a business or start a ministry? The questions and possible answers would play out this way;

What **will** happen if **I quit my job**? I will have more time to build my business or start the ministry. I will miss the privilege to attend the annual managers' conference in

Miami.

What **won't** happen if **I quit my job**? I won't starve since I have saved up enough to sustain my family and I for the next one year.

What **will** happen if I **don't quit my job**? I will continue to feel dissatisfied and unfulfilled.

What **won'**t happen if I **don't quit my job**? I won't start and sustain the business or ministry.

The Cartesian questions open your mind to new alternatives and possibilities. They help you gain clarity on the possibilities presented by your options so that you can make informed decisions. Practice using the Cartesian question often.

After you have made your choice, the next step is to set up a concrete plan to help you accomplish the target. We will see how to effectively plan in the next chapter.

HOW TO MAKE WISE DECISIONS

Decision making is one of the greatest and most important skill that should be taught even from kindergarten!
I look at my life and I can point out few foolish decisions I have made in the past. I'm sure you have bouts of poor decisions in your history too. If we took a moment to be honest with ourselves, we can tell how we arrived at those

poor decisions. Below is a strategic approach for making wise decisions every time.

<u>Objectively seek the facts</u>

Proverbs 18:13 "He who gives an answer before he hears, it is folly and shame to him." (NASB)

I've had moments when I responded before someone got done asking a question. I felt foolish and indeed it was shameful as the scripture above points out.

You are definitely going to regret your decision if you make them before having all the facts possible. I'm not saying you should wait for all eternity but truth is, the people who ask questions find answers.

My 3- watch word for gathering information for a decision making process is **(ASP)**

- **Ask** questions
- **Seek** answers
- **Probe** findings

Never sit down assuming God will always tell you things while you snore at night. Actively seek information.

<u>Play against time</u>

Proverbs 19:2"Enthusiasm without knowledge is no good; haste makes mistakes (NLT)

Wise men play against time; time is never against them! People who are often in a hurry miss it eventually. I understand that there could be moments when we don't have so much time to make a decision. However, one thing I have noticed about the wise is, they are never under pressure because they know how to bring their minds under control when pressure mounts.

The way I do that personally is to say a quick word of prayer, "Father take control". My father taught me to do so while I was in secondary school. It is one of the many powerful things he showed me.

Those three words are effective in the face of any kind of pressure. So if you have very little time to make a decision, don't act in haste. Take a deep breath and say the three power words, **"Father Take control."** These simple words relinquishes your limitations and paves way for the infinite wisdom of the most high. God will help you make the right choice. Remember that He loves us more than we know.

<u>Honour the ultimate priority</u>

1 Corinthians 10:31 "So, whether you eat or drink, or whatever you do, do all to the glory of God." (NASB)

Everyone has priorities that get tested each time they are faced with options. You can decide to make choices that help fulfill your immediate goals; but note that wise people aren't concerned only about now. They think about the future and far into eternity.

To make decisions like the wise, you must always ask yourself, "Would this option glorify God in the end?" Honoring God/Christ is the ultimate priority of the wise.

If an option would not help you achieve that, don't consider it!

<u>Review the past</u>

Proverbs 26:11 "Like a dog that returns to its vomit is a fool who repeats his folly." (NASB)

There is a reason God gave us memories. These memories are not there to torment us but to provide references for us to do better, be better, have better!

I have repeated mistakes in the past but not anymore. I had to hold a board conference with myself and be frank with my soul. I realized that if something failed before, there is a reason it did. I learnt to review my past, find the reasons why things did or didn't work and approached my next opportunities differently. You must find the reasons in your past and modify your behaviour and approaches or else you will get the same failed results due to poor decisions.

Faith doesn't bless your folly! If you made a decision that failed in the past, please don't repeat and expect a miracle. The wise review the past to make better decisions not to repeat mistakes while expecting miracles.

<u>Uphold Integrity</u>

Proverbs 10:9 "He who walks in integrity walks securely, but

he who perverts his ways will be found out."(NASB)

A huge vocabulary in tongue speaking is not synonymous with integrity.

According to Google, integrity is the quality of being honest and having strong moral principles. I'll Like to exchange the word moral for GODLY in that definition. Some people want what they want at all cost. The wise aren't like that.

You can't walk in integrity and fail in life. I didn't say it. The scripture above did. Never compromise your integrity for momentary gain. When faced with options ask yourself, **"Would this decision jeopardize my integrity or hinder my ability to talk to others about Jesus?** Don't sell your generational inheritance for a plate of ijebu garri please!

<u>Seek wise counsel</u>

Proverbs 2:6 "For the Lord gives wisdom; from His mouth comes knowledge and understanding." (NASB)

Yes! The wise seek wise counsel. Wise counsel is found in God's word. Put your butt down and open those pages of the bible for yourself! Look intently into the book of life and seek God's opinion for the matter.

Yeah right! I know there are situations which the bible doesn't expressly address but that is why we have leaders in whom the Spirit of wisdom operates. Ask for their counsel before you make decisions. *"Where no wise guidance is, the people falleth; But in the multitude of counsellors there is safety." Proverbs 11:14 (ASV).*

<u>Follow instruction</u>

Proverbs 19:20 "Hear counsel, and receive instruction, that thou mayest be wise in thy latter end. (KJB)

You can't make wise decisions if you are allergic to instruction. An instruction ignored births your destruction. The next time you have to make a decision. Seek the accompanying instruction! Never assume! SEEK!

7 CHOICES BOUND TO BRING REGRETS

Life is like a menu at a restaurant. You find the familiar, the enticing, the predictable and the completely bland. While you peruse the menu you eventually have to make a choice and then place an order.

The choices we make are like tossing a coin in the air. You can only hope for the side you want to land face up. You are not in total control of what side lands up or down. This uncertainty influences people to choose wisely or foolishly.

Regardless of what menu life offers, below are 7 choices you might plan on making today or are already making that will definitely not favour your chances at fulfillment/happiness (you take your pick) in the future.

1. **The choice to make decisions based on other people's**

opinion

We see things differently and process them differently. Your opinion will definitely be different from another person's. You must be confident enough to view and process issues independently.

Some people can't make decisions until nearly everyone in their lives have approved of it. When you're faced with choices, ask yourself "what do I think?" and not what do people think?

If you keep making choices based on what other people thought? You most likely would have made regrettable choices in the next seven years.

2. **The choice to give up on your dreams to please someone else**

Ever heard the world people pleasers? Pleasing people or getting them to feel comfortable around you is great but not when it is to the detriment of your dreams, vision, calling or purpose.

Some people have spent years at the university studying courses totally opposite to their dreams or desire because they wanted to please their parents. Others have given up their dreams to please a spouse. Irrespective of how logical that choice may seem at the moment, it's bound to evoke regrets years down the line.

3. **The choice to act only when you are surely sure**

Yeah right, no one enjoys making mistakes especially on vital issues of life. However, you can't wait for years trying to be surely sure on a potential spouse, a career path or life's calling. Being surely sure is the practice of waiting really long until you have all the facts, figures and future at the tip of your fingers.

Life never gives us the chance to be surely sure. You will have to make decisions based on the information you have or sometimes based on nothing (visible) but your faith (assuming God is asking you to do something). The problem with waiting to be surely sure is that you most likely will pass on the best while waiting for seven signs and wonders to convince you.

4. **The choice to wait passively for opportunities**

So you hope that someday, someone will invite you to speak at their conference and yet you've never even began to research what aspect of life you will like to become a speaker on. Waiting passively for opportunities to roll by, leaves you lame when the opportunities arrive. If there is something you wish for, prepare like you already know when and how it will happen. Do the opposite and regret will be inevitable.

5. **The choice to settle for less than you deserve**

I'm not the place-yourself-on-an-eternally-high, unreachable pedestal-thinking-person but I definitely believe in reaching for the highest possible quality I desire.

So if you know you're worth better, why pack your bag at your current "location" in life?

If you decide to "manage" what life throws at you without making distinct plans or taking clear steps towards what you deserve or desire, you will definitely regret your laid back approach in years to come.

6. **The choice to be someone you are not**

You know how tempting it is for you to "play along" because you are afraid of losing someone or something you love? Inasmuch as that might seem okay at the moment, it's only a matter of time before those people see you for whom you truly are and they will resent you. Don't try to be someone you are not because you want to get other people to stay with you. No matter the situation, being true to who you are is more honourable than wearing masks around in pretence.

7. **The choice to follow your heart care freely.**

Inasmuch as we gain some sense of satisfaction when we give ourselves what our hearts desire, it is unadvisable to follow your heart care freely. The heart on Its own, can't tell what's totally right or wrong. We have to train/condition it to recognize our idea of wrong or right.

If you do everything your heart desires care freely, you would most likely kill your boss or that friend who snatched your lover. How would you feel after you've killed them? I bet not as good as you envisaged.

Time has a way of placing things in correct perspective. What appears extremely urgent and pressingly important today, may mean absolutely nothing or worthless in seven years time. So rather than act as your heart detects, measure every desire against scripture because in the end, way beyond those seven years in front, what we thought was right won't negate what God's standard of right is.

8

THE POWER OF PLANNING

Meticulous planning will enable everything a man does to appear spontaneous- Mark Cain

Jason Lengstor, a lead developer & architect at IBM says, **"Hope for all the good it brings is a terrible thing to rely on when you have deadlines to meet.** It really just boils down to defining what "success" means in quantifiable terms *before work begins on a project."*

The question I have been asked the most in life is "How old are you?" As a child, nearly every adult I met couldn't hold a conversation with me without asking. "How old are you?" It seemed those words and "How are you?" were the only things adults thought most children could comprehend. You greet an adult in good will and their response turn into an interview. They would ask, how are you? What is your name? How old are you? What class are you? What's the name of your school? They did it in that order so often that I thought adults had a children greetings council that agreed upon the questions they were to ask children.

Did that happen to you? Do you catch yourself doing this to children when you meet them for the first time? Oops, I have caught myself doing that severally

Over the years, "How old are you" has become my all time favourite question because it has the capacity to awaken the desire for growth and development in people.

Every time we tell someone how old we are, there's an unconscious alarm that triggers in our brains. The alarm makes us measure our age against our achievements. This isn't our making. Back then, when you told adults your age, they immediately wanted to know your class at school so they can measure you academic progress against your chronological progress.

One will expect that the age versus class measurement will disappear after graduation. Sadly it doesn't change much. We replace class with other variables such as marriage and financial net worth; such that when you are male and 40, you should at least own a house in your village even if you rent a hut in the city. If you are female and 25, you better be married or have fixed your wedding dates already lest you become the prayer point of friends and family. I still wonder who planned these marital and landlord-ship schedule. When you catch the person, please call me on +234-704-you- really-wanna-call me?

(Laughs)

While we cannot catch whoever set that age mark, we both know that time is priceless and if we must do life successfully? We must understand the value of time.

The very special bank account

Imagine you had a bank account that deposited eighty six thousand and four dollars each morning. The account carries over no balance from day to day, allows you to keep no cash balance, and every evening cancels whatever part of the amount you had failed to use during the day. What would you do? I bet you will withdraw everything first thing in the morning especially when a voice in your head tells you it won't last forever.

  We all have such a bank. Its name is Time. Every morning, it credits you with eighty six thousand and four seconds. Every night it writes off, as lost, whatever time you have failed to use wisely. It carries over no balance from day to day. It allows no overdraft so you can't borrow against yourself or use more time than you have. Each day, the account starts fresh. Each night, it destroys an unused time. If you fail to use the day's deposits, it's your loss and you can't appeal to get it back.[1]

The only way to ensure you make good use of the eighty six thousand and four seconds deposited in your life's account each day is to have a plan.

WHAT IT REALLY MEANS TO PLAN

Have you seen a mad person who is hungry? He sits calmly looking around until the moment he sees someone with the food he desires. He races down, grabs it and runs away.

Though insane, the mad man planned his move. First, he decided to grab someone's food (what), he waited for the food bearer to be distracted (when); he figured what direction to run towards in order to avoid being caught (where). Deciding on what to do, how to do it , where and when to do it are all elements of planning.

Planning is deciding future course of action from amongst alternatives. It is a process that involves **making** and **evaluating** each set of interrelated decisions. **It is selection of missions, objectives and "translation of knowledge into action.** Planning includes the plan, the thought process, action, and implementation. Planning is deciding in advance **what** to do, **how** to do it, **when** to do it, and **who** should do it.[2]

Everyone plans; our plans just don't have the same quality. This is why two people can do the same thing using different plans and they will get different results. If plans are powerful enough to determine outcomes, then planning is a skill everyone should acquire.

Many people think effective planning applies to corporate organizations alone. Effective planning applies largely to our personal lives also. One of the most effective ways to be successful at who you are called to be and what you are called to do, is to see, treat yourself and function as an organization. For instance, an organization has clear goals and strategies enshrined in her mission and vision statement. You should have same for your personal life. Do you have goals for your life? Do you have a mission and vision statement?

THE PLANNING PROCESS

Patrick Montana and Bruce Charnov outline a three-step result-oriented process for planning: [3]

1. **Choosing a destination**: What is the goal? What do you want to achieve?
2. **Evaluating alternative routes:** If I did A would I get to the chosen destination? Would B better and why?
3. **Deciding the specific course of your plan:** I will do B using this by xyz time.

If you like a simple, easy to remember planning process go with Montana and Charnov but if you are like me who likes a bit of details especially if it will help me understand better, see this 7 step planning process below

1. **Identify your goal:** The goal is the big picture. The result you want in the end. What you want to achieve, do or become.

2. **Set the objectives:** The objectives are the end result of your activities. It must be measurable and related to the expected result.

3. **Develop premises:** Premises refer to making assumptions regarding the future. What will or will not happen if I did A or didn't do A?

4. **List the various alternatives for achieving the objectives.** For example, if the objective is to increase the length of time you spend praying from 10 to 40 minutes daily, then the prayer time can be increased through
   a. Not watching TV before you go to bed
   b. Using a prayer book
   c. Praying in the spirit for the first 15 minutes.
   d. Singing Worship songs after each prayer point.

5. **Evaluate the various alternatives:** Note the pros and cons of each of the alternatives you listed.

6. **Select an alternative**: Then, eliminate those with more cons and select those with more pros and feasibility. The most feasible alternative is the one that is most profitable to your goal and has the least negative consequences. The selected alternative or alternatives become your main plan. However, you will need to map out smaller plans from this main plan. These smaller plans are called supportive plans.[4]
   For instance, If the alternative routes you chose above were to use a prayer book and not watch TV before going to bed, the supportive plan could include, to

buy a specific prayer book and unplug the TV in your room, one hour before bed time

7. **Implement the plan:** Start doing what you have decided to do (I will show you how to take action in the next chapter)

THE OBJECTIVE OF PLANNING

The objective of planning is a specific result that a person or system aims to achieve within a time frame and with available resources.[5]

Some examples of planning objectives include,

To increase my income by three hundred percent (desired achievement or aim), between January 2019 and December 2019 (time frame) using my graphic design, public speaking and editorial skills (available resources).

To deepen my relationship with God (desired achievement or aim) between April 2019 and May 2019 (time frame) using online bible study materials and my pastor's weekly sermons (available resources).

Therefore, planning is the process of breaking your goals into objectives.

THE DIFFERENCE BETWEEN OBJECTIVES AND GOALS

It has been said that Goals without objectives can never be achieved while objectives without goals will never get you to where you want to be. Indeed the two concepts are related and yet separate.[4]

Goals

Goals are long-term aims that you want to achieve. A *goal* is an idea of the future or desired result that a person or a group of people envisions, plans and commits to achieve.[5]

Objectives

Objectives are concrete outcomes that can be grasped by following specific steps. Objectives are concrete in statement and purpose. It doesn't leave room for you to wonder if they've been achieved or not. When you nail it, you know that you have.

Below is a table by investor words, showing elaborate differences between goals and objectives.

	GOALS	OBJECTIVE
Definition	Something which you try to achieve	A specific result that a person or system aims to achieve within a time frame and with available resources.
Time Frame	Usually long-term.	A series of smaller steps, often along the way to achieving a

		long-term goal.
Magnitude.	Typically involves life changing outcomes, like retiring, buying a home or making a major career change.	Usually a near-term target of a larger expected outcome, such as passing a course as part of completing a degree program.
Outcome of immediate.	Actions tend to advance progress in a very general sense; there is often awareness that there are several ways to reach a goal, so specific outcomes aren't necessary.	Very specific and measurable, a target is established and victory is declared only when the target is hit.
Purpose of action	A goal is often characterized as a change of direction that will ultimately lead to a desired	Objectives tend to be actions aimed at accomplishing a certain task.

	outcome.	
Example	"I want to retire by age 50	In order to reach my goal of retiring at age 50, I need to save $20,000 by the end of this year"
Hierarchy	Goals tend to control objectives; a change in a goal could eliminate one or more objectives, or add new ones.	An objective can modify a goal, but will seldom change it in a fundamental way, even if the objective isn't reached.

From the table above, we see that both goals and objectives are directed towards results and are at different but related scope in any mission.

SHOULD YOU HAVE A LIFE PLAN?

You must have heard of the popular 5-year personal plan, where one has clear goals mapped out for the next 5 years of their life.

While majority of people talk about it (talkers), only few people actually have a 5-year plan for their lives (doers). The others believe we don't need to plan as such since God's will prevails (nay-sayers). Which of these categories do you fall into?

Whichever category you are in represents your approach to life planning. While I respect your approach, the one question I need you to answer for yourself sincerely is, how has my approach to life planning facilitated my success?

You can determine that by looking at the quality of your life and level of productivity in the last five years. Would the quality of your life and level of productivity be excellent, if you rated them on a scale of 0-10?

If you got a 10 being a talker or nay-sayer, then don't bother about a life plan. You are doing just great. However, I guarantee that your life will exceedingly improve if you had a life plan compared to when you don't.

Having a life plan does not in any way mean that you don't trust God. It doesn't mean that you have set your heart to oppose the will of God for your life. Having a life plan means that you are responsible enough to intentionally strive towards accomplishing what God has revealed to you at that time.

If you are a believer, you already know that God orders your step into the culmination/fulfillment of his purpose for your life. However, God doesn't lead us in a blindfolded state. While he may leave out details of the process to us, He often shares the grand purpose with us and gives us specific instruction on how to fulfill the grand purpose. It is from this instruction, that we are expected to develop our life plans in order to accomplish the grand purpose.

<u>See this case study below</u>

Tobi Afolayan (imaginary person) was trained as an IT engineer and has over eight years work experience with major Telecom organizations in Nigeria. Tobi recently got saved and eventually learnt that his purpose is to bring order into people's lives. After a couple of years, Tobi gets an impression to start a software development company. At first he thought it was his ambition, because he was raised to think God only sends people to open churches and host revival meetings. He soon realizes it was God leading him to start that company when after three months of starting the company (obedience), he realizes that many young people suddenly look up to him for direction and mentorship. He starts getting speaking invites from both religious and non-religious youth-focused organizations to come address young people.

As the platforms increased, the timid Tobi gradually disappears, giving rise to the bold, confident Tobi who now graces international platforms as a public speaker.

One day, Tobi gets another strong impression to begin hosting mentorship programs for aspiring IT experts within ages 17 and 35. He also gets an impression to include a curriculum that addresses the human need for a divinely led life.

Tobi struggles with this for two weeks because he is afraid that the curriculum doesn't tally with industry practices. He tries to wave it aside but it keeps coming strongly. He then decides to follow the impression.

He begins the mentoring program and within six weeks of participating, protégés testify that their lives are more organized, they know what to do with their dreams now, they are more productive, they are able to operate efficiently.

Since testimonies are a reflection of what it means to have order in one's life, Tobi is consequently fulfilling the grand purpose of God for his life. This is also what it means to execute missions effectively.

For Tobi to successfully arrive at this point, he had plans. These plans were drawn from two instructions which God impressed in his heart at two different points.

The first instruction was that he starts a software development company. To achieve that goal, Tobi needed to have a plan. The plan will include, decisions about what kind of software, the location of the company, the capital needed and how to raise it, the kind of people (and their qualifications) needed on his team.

It takes a clear plan consisting of goals and objectives to start and build a successful software company. If Tobi didn't have a plan, years would go by and all Tobi would be saying is, *"I want to start a software company"* but would never begin.

The second instruction was that he should begin a mentorship program that included a curriculum that addresses the need for a divinely led life. If there is anything in the world that requires planning, it is developing a curriculum. Tobi will never run the mentorship program if he didn't plan.

These plans could have been stretched over a two year or five year course. The duration is only as it is necessary for Tobi to achieve the goals of starting a software company and a mentorship programme effectively.

At the time when Tobi got those impressions and made those plans, they became his life plans.

A Life plan has a powerful way of motivating you to make progress because it helps you define where you are going (goal/ destination), what to do, how to do it, when to do it, and who should do it.

If we were privileged to look into Tobi's planner at the time (February 2016) he got the impression to start the company, it will look something like this.

Goal: To start a software company which develops operating systems by the year 2019

Objective 1: To identify the loop holes (desired achievement) in Android, Linux, macOs, IOS and windows using online survey tools (available resources) on Google before June 2017 (time frame).

Objective 2: To develop an improved version of the best among them using a team of software development experts before November 2017.

You can see that having a clear goal and written objectives (plan) empowers you to fulfill purpose effectively. Would you rather not have a life plan?

WHY YOU SHOULD CONSCIOULSY PLAN EVERY ASPECT OF YOUR LIFE

Clear Direction: Planning helps you decide on where you are going and how to get there. You will be able to easily evaluate opportunities and activities to see which is pivotal or not to achieving your goal .

Increased efficiency: If you don't plan you will waste time, money, energy and otherwise profitable idea on events and activities that gets you nowhere.

Risk control: Planning prompts you to look into the future (forecasting). It makes you take necessary precautions to prepare for future uncertainties in advance.

Effective co-ordination: One of the red flags of disorderliness is absence of planning. You don't want to live your life in a way that life happens to you. You are the one to happen to life. Planning directs aspects of your life to seamlessly reflect your purpose.

Motivation: One of the reasons people fail at mission, is lack of motivation. Planning motivates you to move forward because you can see the small and big picture.

THE FIVE REASONS PLANS FAIL
AND HOW TO PREVENT THAT

Planning Fallacy: If you have ever underestimated the length of time it will take you to complete a task? Then you've been a victim of planning fallacy.

Planning fallacy is a situation where one underestimates the time required to get something done. We often don't realize that there could be delays or snags when we set out to accomplish something. Every time you think about a task without considering the possible delays that may arise, you become susceptible to planning fallacy.

For instance, if you had an event scheduled for 10am and you live 30 minutes away from the venue, you may plan to get done with bathing, cooking and cleaning between the hours of 6am and 8am, do a few other things and leave home at 9:30am.

Two hours allocated to chores sounds like a good time to your mind until you realize that it is 9am and you are still cleaning. You end up leaving at 10am and arriving at 10:40am due to an unexpected traffic jam.

In such instance, your plan to arrive at 10am, failed due to planning fallacy. You underestimated the length of time required to complete the tasks of bathing, cleaning, cooking, laundry and driving to the event.

The best way to prevent failed plans caused by planning fallacy, is to make room for snags or delays when you apportion time to your tasks. If a task would usually take 10 minutes, allocate 20 minutes to it. If it would usually take 2 weeks, allocate 3 weeks to it. That way, you will be able to reach your goals in time.

Planning with no intention to follow through: If you have to plan anything, make up your mind to pull through with the plan. Avoid making plans for the sake of having a plan. You are not making plans to impress anyone. You make plans to achieve a goal. If your goal is to finish preparing for a presentation within seven days, and your plan includes spending the first two days researching? Follow through with the plan.

Partial commitment to your goal: My most important goal in life is to hear these words when I finally appear before the Lord, "Weldone Annie, **you finished**". Those two words written in bold are my greatest ambition/goal/focus. Therefore when I encounter hitches as I go about implementing the plans drawn for fulfilling the mission assigned to me, I remember this grand goal to which I am fully committed. Plans will fail if you are not totally committed to your goal. How badly do you want it? How badly, my dear?

Wrong relationships: Some plans require that you work with people. To avoid stories that touch the heart, it is very important that you select people with the right skills, exposure and wisdom required to implement the plan. Sentiments would be your biggest foe when building a team.

Don't let it cloud your sense of judgment. Having the wrong set of people can make a perfect plan flop on a grand scale.

Rigidity: This is the inability or unwillingness to adapt or adjust to change. When you made your plan, you certainly did to the best of your knowledge at that time. However, if during implementation you realize that the information you had earlier is no longer valid, adjust your plans to accommodate the change. Failure to do so, would lead to a failed plan.

Ignoring history: Like the writer says in the book of Ecclesiastes, nothing is new under the sun. There is a hundred percent chance that someone has done or attempted what you plan to do. This is why research is very important. Dig into the past. Find out what they did that worked, or didn't. Find out how you can improve on the past and include your findings in the plan.

God's sovereignty: No matter how smart we are, we will be dumb to overrule the truth that God sits in heaven and rules in the affairs of men. The beauty about the sovereignty of God is that He always gives us bigger and better than we planned for ourselves. If you've done all the right things that you could and should have done and a plan still didn't work out, it might just be that God is conditioning the universe to bring you something way better than you could have got yourself.

9

THE POWER OF ACTION

A good plan violently executed now is better than a perfect plan executed next week. George S. Patton

Growing up, I noticed my father saw lots of Chinese movies. There was always a scene to show off karate moves to the amazement of the audience. Jet Li, Bruce Lee and Jackie Chan were the heroes of such movies. Every time one of these men landed a stifling kick on their opponent, my dad would shout, "action!"

For a ninety-minute movie, you would hear more than one hundred "action!" from my dad. For years, I thought action meant slamming an opponent with a powerful Jackie Chan kick. Please don't laugh at my ignorance.

Come to think of it, wouldn't it be great to be able to slam projects with some quick, powerful, effective Karate kick? That's what I will like to help you achieve at this point in the book.

WHAT IT MEANS TO TAKE ACTION

The word action (noun)

- Is the fact or process of doing something typically to achieve an aim (Oxford)
- The process of doing something, especially when dealing with a problem or difficulty (Cambridge)
- Doing something for a particular purpose (Collins)

Did you notice how the word **doing** keeps showing up?
You can't talk about action in your dreams or imaginary world. Your witty idea, brilliant plan, anointing, gifts or burning desire is all air without any **doing**.

Taking action requires you to start doing. Get off your dream or imaginary life and start implementing your plans and if you have no plans yet but know what you want, mapping a plan is also an action at that level. So go ahead and map out your plans using the techniques I shared with you earlier. You might even be uncertain about the authenticity of your plans but don't let that hinder you from doing. Like Philip Sydney says, "Start where you are, use what you have and do what you can."

Perhaps you desire better grades at school. Rather than sit there feeling like a failure, focus on the current term or semester **(start where you are)** and plug into past questions, library resource, excelling classmates **(use what you have)** and read what you've got one page at a time **(do what you can).**

The same goes for finding a spouse, landing a better job, starting or growing your business or finally hosting that training (God asked you to run for teenagers five years ago) you have been feeling too inadequate to begin.

The most common problem with people God asked to begin hosting an event is that they are waiting till they can afford a high brow event center with powerful AC and made in heaven fragrance. I'm sorry to say you most likely would wait forever especially if you don't have the finances yet to fund that.

A good example of starting where you are would be to host the event on social media. Hosting a social media event saves you the cost of renting a space. You have a smart phone right? You have whatsapp, Instagram and facebook installed right? If you answered yes to any of these, you already have something to use. Therefore go ahead and do what you can.

It really breaks my heart when young people do nothing about an instruction God gave them several years after. I'm a strong believer of learning on the job. I will rather begin working on a ministry assignment with little competence than wait ten years to gain competence to begin.   The person that started with the little they know would gain mastery quickly, be recognized by many and eventually become trusted by public over the years. In the course of those ten years, he/she would have gained both theoretical and practical knowledge while all you would have is theory. Who has theory helped?

I keep saying this, timing is very important as you go about your life's mission. Stop waiting and take action already!

The clause, "I only have one life to live" shouldn't apply only when you want to indulge yourself with the luxuries of life. You should apply that to every God breathed instruction. Treat your purpose and the assignment with a lot more urgency than you do other aspects of your life.

THE MARSHMALLOW EXPERIMENT

Tom Wujec, author and fellow at Autodesk, presented at TED 2010. He shared with us how he conducted a team building experiment with people from various works of life. He got MBA holders, top business executives such as CEOs and the likes, students, designers, architects all the way to kindergarten pupils.

The various groups were given one yard of string, one yard of tape, twenty sticks of spaghetti and a marshmallow. They all had eighteen minutes to build a free standing structure using the string, tape, sticks of spaghetti and marshmallow. Most teams spent more time planning their structures and couldn't finish building before time ran out. For those who eventually finished, the spaghetti skyscraper came crashing the moment they placed the marshmallow on it. Meanwhile, the kindergarten pupils started building immediately. Their structure fell each time they placed the marshmallow at the top but they simply noted that as one of the ways it wouldn't work. They kept trying and in the end, they finished in time with the tallest, firmest spaghetti structure.

Wujec says business school graduates approached the task by applying what they are taught in graduate school, which is to seek out and execute the one correct solution; while kindergarten pupils simply built, tested and repeated the process until they built a structure that worked.

This just goes a long way to buttress how taking action would always be better than moving things in your head.

WHAT DO YOU NEED TO BUILD WITH THE SPAGHETTI, STRINGS AND TAPES IN YOUR LIFE?

How many achievements have you missed because you have been waiting for that one strategy that works? How many quality women have slipped off your grip because you were waiting for the perfect line with which to ask them out? How many business idea have drowned in the crevice of your heart because you are waiting for a sure fire way to begin? How many books have disappeared from your mind because you were waiting to be an authority first before getting published? Get up, Get started and learn on the job!

I can relate with your inhibitions if you are not a high risk taker. I'm not a high risk taker. I am one of those people who like some relative level of certainty before I plunge my resources into any course. I understand that it is not easy for our type to just take uncalculated risks in the name of taking action. However, I have never allowed my inhibition to hold me spell bound that I take no action at all towards my goals. You mustn't allow that too.

You've spent several years researching how to start a business, how to write a book, how to be a world class chef, how to play the piano, how to start an NGO, how to run a school, how to host a youth conference. You've given motivational speakers thousands of naira or dollars attending "how to become what you want" trainings but you've never done one thing with all the information you have been paying heavily to get. When would you use all that information to build your life? When would you get to work? Remember, start where you are, use what you have and do what you can. If you don't get it right the first time, you would only have learnt one not so great way to go about the mission. The timer has begun. Start building what you have to build already!

WHY YOU HAVEN'T TAKEN ACTION

It will hurt me deeply if I found that you read this book and tossed it aside without **doing** anything towards executing the mission in your heart. To prevent that from happening, I will like us to look at the most common reasons why people don't take action. Hopefully, you will find which one applies to you and we can journey towards your Jackie Chan moments in life.

Pleasure versus Pain Preference:

There is that basic instinct in man that makes us prefer pleasure over pain. I mean, why wake up when a little more sleep feels good? Why drink warm water on a sunny day when cold water feels good? Why fast when a well prepared, steamy inviting meal sits on the dining table on a Monday morning? These examples are the everyday realities we face in the pleasure versus pain challenge.

You also might have noticed that your desire to avoid pain is stronger than your desire to feel pleasure even if that pain will eventually bring pleasure. For example, there are adults who will rather self medicate than get proper medical attention at a hospital because they don't want an injection. They are aware that the temporal pain of a piercing needle will bring them relief and consequently the pleasure of living in their bodies, yet they will avoid injections.

Could it be that you are considering the pain you might have to endure should you decide to take action? Despite knowing that the pain is going to eventually birth your pleasure, why haven't you decided to begin the journey and embrace the pain already? You haven't because you are still operating based on the basic human instinct. You can't take action if you allow your preference for pleasure or fear of pain to overrule your desire to see the manifestation of your goals and vision.

One way to subdue your preference of pleasure and fear of pain is to focus on the greater pleasure and the greater pain.

For a sick patient as we saw earlier, he/she needs to compare the pleasure of avoiding a needle pierce against the pleasure of a healthy body. He/she needs to compare the pain of a needle pierce against the pain of losing his/her life as a result of the illness. The easiest way is to draw up a table and insert your options as seen below.

Lesser pain	Greater Pain
Take the injection	May lose an organ, may die
Lesser pleasure	**Greater pleasure**
Escape the injection	Recover faster and carry on with my life

Placing things in a table makes reasoning easier. On a lighter note, you probably didn't see any sense in those statistics classes in senior secondary school where you were taught to represent data using bar charts, pie charts and table's right? At least you now know your mathematics teacher was useful afterall.

Think about times when you took action for something that was important to you despite having to endure the initial pain. You either subconsciously focused on the greater pleasure you wished to attain or the greater pain you wished to avoid.

Read the book **7 signs you are sabotaging your future**, I shared applicable steps on how you can put your love for pleasure under check in order to live the productive life you were born for. You should also get the 7 signs workbook, there is help with excessive love of pleasure in there.

Survival instinct (SI):

If you think this instinct was only in Esau? Think again. It's in every one of us. While you may not have sold your birthright right (yet or never), you have probably had moments when you told yourself, "I have to be alive today before I can talk about tomorrow", right? If you have ever said that to yourself or anyone and made a decision based on that, you've operated based on the survival instinct.

Underneath every decision made based on the survival instinct, is the fear of death. I'm sure you know it is not only humans that die; situations, dreams and projects die too. Hence, we sometimes fear the death of our current situations. Let's zoom into the life of this imaginary pretty girl called Nkechi.

Nkechi strongly desires to earn more. She hopes to use her extra income to begin a school for children with special needs. Her current job neither gives her time to take on added responsibilities that could bring her more income to begin her school nor does it provide a structure were she can possibly climb up the ladder of the organization in order to earn more.

Nkechi strongly desires to start this school not only because God has communicated his plans to use her to empower these children, but also because she knows that she will eventually earn more by running such business. Despite knowing that the special needs children school is both a divine mandate/mission and a lucrative business idea, Nkechi has decided to stay in her current job because *"a bird at hand is worth ten in the bush."*

While Nkechi can resign and hop on to a better paying job, she hasn't found any better paying job since the past three years that she has been searching. Rather than look out for other ways by which she can get this school to manifest, she waves the dream aside saying, "If it is God? He will make it happen". Nkechi packed the mandate at a garage because she is afraid of death-the loss of her job.

How many mandates have you neglected simply because you are afraid of pain and would rather cling to the current pleasure? How many dreams have you aborted because you allowed your survival instinct to blind your eyes and mind from recognizing opportunities that could make the dream move from paper to play out? Are you like Nkechi who thinks," if it is God? He will make it happen", therefore I can sit in my comfort zone and wait till God throws the resources in my laps?

Snap off that illusion, my dear. Snap off that illusion. If you don't dare your SI, dreams will continue to die in your hands, missions will continue to fail at your watch, nations will continue to suffer due to your negligence, your multi-million dollar companies will never see daylight, you will never marry the man or woman of your dreams. Is that how you really want to live your life?

The survival instinct is also the reason many people will never take action concerning their poverty level. SI will convince you that you have to eat all you earn. It will make you believe you could die saving only for someone else to take all the money.

In what ways is SI holding you back from taking action? Could it be the reason you have never started any of the businesses you dream about? Could it be the reason you have not enrolled for your MBA or that professional course, preferring to spend the money on everyday life instead of saving up or doing things to earn more so you can afford the course? Is your survival instinct preventing you form taking action towards fulfilling your purpose?

One way to put the survival instinct under check is to answer this question honestly. Would I be fulfilled on the long run, if I took no action towards my purpose, calling, and goal? If you answered yes, do nothing; but if you answered no, then you must dare your survival instinct, take action and embrace the ultimate fulfillment that you deserve to experience at the end of your life.

Analysis Paralysis

"If you spend too much time thinking about a thing, you'll never get it done." Says Bruce Lee.
Little wonder his brutal karate kicks land so well on his opponent that my dad couldn't help but shout, "Action!"
I thought I heard you say you were thinking about starting an importation business. What happened to that thought? What did you do about it? I thought I heard you say you will start an online class for upcoming make-up artistes. What happened to that thought? What have you done about it? Wasn't it two years ago that you thought about opening a blog to share your writings and inspire people who are going through a divorce? You are still thinking twenty four whole

months after. You need some laying on of sense, my love.

Analysis Paralysis has invaded you and you've lost the will for action. Too much thinking and excessive analysis, mess with your power to take action. Be like Bruce Lee. Don't think about how the kick will land. Just roll your hands like you are drawing a flyer in the air, shout yourself to full energy, lift yourself off your sorry state and kick the heck out of your mission now!

I completely agree with Derek Rydall who says, " It's easy to travel through our mind and think we've gotten somewhere, setting bold intentions that lead to little or no action but give us the feeling of doing something climbing the mountaintop of inspired ideas before falling back into the valley of mediocrity. We can seem so decisive in our thoughts, but unless it's followed up by action, it's just self-indulgence and wishful thinking."[1]

Stop thinking about going back to school. Get out there and apply for an admission already. Stop thinking about getting married propose to her already. Stop thinking about organizing a visit to the orphanage get it done already! Stop thinking about how the company will respond to your proposal, send them the proposal already! Stop wondering if anyone will sign up for your coaching services, make the announcement already! Stop wondering if your marriage can still be saved; send him/her the love note and gift regardless!

In what aspect of life is analysis paralysis stopping you from taking action? It's okay to drop this book down right now and go get it done. Deciding to do it is not enough. Like Tony Robbins says, "a real decision is measured by the fact that you've taken new action." What new action were you supposed to take on that mission, last year?

inertia (ĭ-nûr'shə)
This is the tendency of a body to resist acceleration; the tendency of a body at rest to remain at rest or of a body in motion to stay in motion in a straight line unless acted on by an outside force. (dictionary.com)

Every day, purpose tugs your heart in the direction of the problem you were created to solve. Rather than move with the momentum of its pull, you sit waiting for a thunder-like-voice declaring "thus says the Lord".

How long are you going to keep waiting for stars to fall off the sky as sign before you believe that God is calling you to fix an issue for nations?

You've remained in a state of inertia, waiting for someone to come echo the same things God has been speaking to you about. We call it waiting for a sign? What confirmation are you waiting for, when you've already heard the Lord tell you, you've even had dreams and seen visions, you've got a clear word from the bible confirming all of that and the burden of the situation rests heavily on your soul? You still want a sign? Are you Gideon? (Judges 6-8).

Look love, God responded to Gideon's fleece test because in that dispensation, Gideon hadn't the Holyghost to help him grasp the mind of the father (God); but you (as a believer in Christ Jesus) have the Holyghost (You and Gideon are not in the same class. John 16:3 says, *"But when He the Sprit of Truth, comes, **he will guide you into all the truth**.*

He will not speak on His own; He will speak only what He hears, and He will tell you what is yet to come."(NIV).

Did you see that? That's why you've been praying. "God if this is your will let my phone ring now. God, if this is your will, let it rain tonight" and nothing happens afterwards!

Huh? Are you serious? Come on now, God is not going to play test and see with you. He has given you a word and remember that a word is enough for the wise. Are you wise?

Get off that state of inertia darling! Just stop already. Stop waiting for someone abroad to help you. Stop waiting for the government to invite you over. How can anyone find you to help if you haven't even made a move towards the mission in the first place?

Infobesity

The creative coinage *infobesity* is a blend based on the words information and obesity - the condition of being overweight in a way which is unhealthy.

Infobesity is the condition of continually consuming large amounts of information, especially when this has a negative effect on a person's well-being and ability to concentrate (Macmillan). We live in an age where information about anything imaginable is available. We are constantly pumped with information from television, radio, bill boards, books and our smart phones. Look around you this minute, except you are in a mortuary, there must be new information coming to your mind right now or an old information having a repeat entrance into your mind.

The modern term for infobesity is information overload.

You are in this condition if you have books you have never opened on your phone, emails you have signed up for that you have never read, classes you enrolled for that you have never attended, Programs you have recorded on your DSTV Decoder that you have never had the time to catch up with. It's really not your fault. It is the age we live in. We are being told more than we can handle. Social media doesn't help either. If we avoid the television or radios, the news is waiting right on our phones for us.

The problem with this is many people spend forever researching on a project but never begin the project. Sometimes, when you know too much about something, it becomes really difficult for you to make a rational decision. Haven't you had a time when you had to choose and because you had too many options to choose from, you could hardly pick any? You probably beckoned on someone to help you choose because you couldn't trust your over informed mind.

How long have you been researching on how to run a business, how to start a ministry and never getting close to starting?

Your head is filled with facts and figures dating back to year nineteen-before-the-earth-was-formed that you have become the climate predictor of your own destiny. You are able to now tell what year is best for you to begin the mission. 2015 was not good enough to begin because you were in school, 2016 was not good enough because you got married. 2017 was not good enough because hurricane sweep-the-world hit your father's compound; even 2019 is still not good enough because you have just had a baby.

My dear, infobesity is preventing you. You know too much that you cannot subdue yourself enough to take action for the mission. You think time is waiting for you right? This year is because you had a baby, next year it will be because you had twins. The year after that will be because the kids are schooling or because the things you read have expired so you need to go for a new training. Keep training, you hear? Don't use the one you've gathered so far. Are you enjoying being infobesed? You've researched enough! It is time to take action on the mission!

When you catch yourself saying, "I don't' know where to begin, I don't know enough yet, I'm too overwhelmed to start at this point, someone is already doing it," there is a ninety percent chance that you are struggling with infobesity.

While information overload looks like an inevitable state, it is actually evitable. You have the power to shut down all information channels and give your mind a break from all the valid and invalid noise. You can shut down the TV for a week, you can stay off social media for a week or more-no posting, no surfing through anyone's wall, no email checking or sending. Just you being truly present in your environment and focusing on what is most important to you. I did this last weekend and I didn't feel like it should end. It wasn't just a personal retreat. It was a time of refreshing for my mind, body and soul. You should try it out.

Limiting Beliefs

A limiting belief is a conviction you hold as true about yourself, about others, or about the world that prevents you from being something, doing something you otherwise would have done.

Limiting beliefs can be subtle. They often require bulb moments for their bearer to realize, "this is what has been holding me back all these years."

Do you believe that the business will fail if you started without a master degree? Do you believe you won't get seed funds because you are not connected to the high and mighty in the industry? Do you believe that you cannot serve successfully in ministry because no one in your family has ever done that? Do you believe you will never find love because your marriage just ended in a brutal divorce? You believe you can't run a ministry effectively because you are single? If you answered yes to any of these questions, then that is one of the reasons you have not taken action about the related area of your life.

One very common limiting belief that most people have but don't realize is the belief that they can't do anything about their situation or purpose because they lack motivation. That's a big lie but because they believe it, they cannot take action until someone or something happens to motivate them.

Your mission is too priceless for you to will over the power to take action to some external motivation. What if no one ever motivates you? What if that special occasion never comes? You can't afford to wait forever.

I've found that motivation is the result of action not the cause of an action. You don't need to wait to feel high/motivated/inspired in order to land the mission a knock out kick. Will yourself to raise your leg high up in the sky and land it on the target; you will be motivated to do it again.

Limiting beliefs are usually experiential-evidence based. Your mind is convinced about them because you have had an experience that impressed them strongly on your heart.

I agree with Dunja Rado an intuitive mentor and coach who says, "The essence of a limiting belief is emotion. It is not a thought, it is an emotion. "

On her blog (BeBee Producer), Dunja explains that humans develop limiting beliefs when they experience an overwhelming emotion. For instance, if you just started learning to drive and had an accident? The **experience** (accident) will ignite a deep **emotion** (fear) in your heart. Accident then serves as evidence which your mind holds in conviction that you are a bad driver. Every time you have to drive, you see the emotion of fear taking over your mind to re-iterate the belief that you are a bad driver and consequently, you will have another accident as a result of the emotion (fear). Some people never drive again after an accident. Others have been able to break off the limiting belief fueled by their experiential-evidence and have moved on to become car racers. Am I communicating?

Limiting beliefs are disempowered when we challenge the evidence surrounding that belief. That's what we are going to do next.

IDENTIFYING AND DISEMPOWERING LIMITING BELIEFS

Now, spare me a moment to walk you through identifying and disempowering one limiting belief that has prevented you from taking action through the years? Get a note book you care about and a pen that looks just fine.

Identify that **one thing you want done** in the next 2 weeks. It could be to finally start your business, launch the online magazine or begin the youth prayer group. Whatever it is, write it down.

Identify and write out all the limiting beliefs (you can think about) that have stopped you from taking action all along. Examples, I don't have enough capital, I don't know much of the bible yet, I am a bad driver, I can't teach.

Pick one of those limiting belief. Decide on the one you feel is the strongest and let's **Identify** and **challenge the evidence** surrounding that belief using these questions.

Identify: Why do I believe this? (Write this down)
Perhaps your answer is because you failed, or didn't have a mother to guide you, or because your teacher never praised you.
Challenge: What other areas of my life have I achieved something despite the situation (**experiential-evidence)** that has made me believe (**insert limiting belief**) about myself?

The goal here is to create doubts in your heart concerning the limiting belief. Once you can doubt it, you dispel its power over you and embrace an opportunity to replace those beliefs with a better version that empowers you to take action. See Ada's note below to help you understand this exercise better.

The one action Ada desires to take is to lunch a master class that teaches nursing mothers to study the bible. The limiting belief she is trying to disempower is "I'm a bad teacher"

In **identifying the evidence**, Ada has why do I believe I am a bad teacher?

- My daughter says I am a bad teacher
- When I taught in the past, the students didn't understand easily.

In **challenging the evidence**, Ada has

- My daughter says I am a bad teacher
  - Does my daughter know what makes a good teacher?
  - What else does my daughter tells me that is incorrect?
  - Does my daughter sometimes tell me that she has learnt something (perhaps not related to her homework) from me?
  - Has anyone else ever learnt anything from me?

- When I taught in the past, the students didn't understand easily.
    - How many times have I explained something to someone this week and they understood?
    - Were there any other influences that made the students not understand easily? Was I impatient? Was I tired? Were they distracted?

Identifying the experiential evidences that fuels an emotion and supports a limiting belief, gives you the power to break free and update those beliefs. Get the picture?

Now that you understand better repeat the exercise above on a fresh sheet of paper. When you are done, update your beliefs. Here is how to update limiting beliefs.

UPDATING LIMITING BELIEFS

To update a limiting belief, you only need to
1. Use words to invoke a positive emotion when you think about the activity.
2. Use words to bring your mind to focus on the action you need to take.
3. Powerfully declare that you take action.

Still using Ada as an example, haven questioned her limiting beliefs, Ada must have realized that things are not as they seem.

- At 6, her daughter can't possibly know all of what makes a good teacher.

- She is not a bad teacher just because her daughter says so; afterall there are other things her daughter has said that were not true.
- Her daughter has told her she learnt to sing "Oluwa e tobi" (a Yoruba worship song) from her. Therefore anyone can learn anything from her.
- Other people have learnt several things from her. She taught her niece to make pap. She taught her four year old to button his shirt properly. She taught her husband to play candy crush.
- She has explained something to two clients twice at the bank (where she works) this week and they understood.
- She realized the students she taught during her pre-university days were distracted and she didn't feel bold enough to caution them during her classes.

Armed with these perspective towards her limiting belief, Ada can update **"I am a bad teacher"** with **"I am an excellent teacher (invokes a happy emotion) who simply needs to capture the attention of my students and I do."**

Noticed two things here?

Firstly, this updated belief, evokes a positive emotion within her. Thinking of herself as an excellent teacher evokes happiness as opposed to the emotion she will feel when she thinks of herself as a bad teacher.

Secondly, it brings her mind to focus on the action (capture my students attention) she needs to take to become a better teacher.

Thirdly, she declares that she does capture her students' attention.

For an updated belief to work, you must truly believe it.

The mind is programmed logically and the heart is programmed emotionally. That is why I didn't tell you to go about declaring "I am not a bad teacher" which definitely won't work because your mind is still hearing and consequently focusing on the term bad nor did I say you should just start declaring "I am a good teacher"; which won't work either if you did not challenge the evidences that convinced you to believe otherwise.

I took the time to guide you to identify the evidences surrounding your limiting beliefs so that you can readily believe your updated version.

Now go ahead and declare the updated version out loudly. If you were Ada, you should say this out loud, **"I am an excellent teacher (invokes a happy emotion) who simply needs to capture the attention of my students and I do."**

Next, Ada starts her master class teaching people how to study the bible **(action taken)**. She **recognizes evidences** to back up her new belief and she **records them** as her **reality**.

Go take action on the goal you identified above and kick it within the next two weeks. Just in case you still don't realize how those limiting beliefs held you back, here is a story as told by Christopher Delaney of Employment King,

"Before 1945 people believed that you could not run a mile in under 4 minutes, this was a belief that everyone shared which meant it was an easy belief to back up with evidence (other people and athletes telling you – your evidence does not need to be true for you to use it to back up your belief) people tried and failed. In 1945 Roger Banister ran a mile in under 4 minutes instantly breaking that belief, the following year 37 other runners ran a mile in under 4 minutes – that's the power of beliefs".

BECOME AN ACTION TAKER

Like Jackie Chan, Jet Li and Bruce Lee, action is taken when you land a powerful kick on your target. Therefore, the only way to become an action taker is to actually land those kicks! Are you ready to land heroic kicks on your target? Then you must keep this in mind- The best way to take action is to take action!

10

THE POWER OF CONSISTENCY

What is consistent in your life, is your life- Abdul Rauf

The Chinese Bamboo Tree

Have you heard of the Chinese bamboo tree? Like other plants, it requires nurturing – water, fertile soil, good doze of sunshine. While the farmer invests all of those, the Chinese bamboo tree shows no visible sign of growth in its first year. One would expect that while it takes most plants three to five days to sprout above the soil, twelve months should be enough for the Chinese bamboo to give the farmer some good sign. Instead of germinating in its first year, the tree requires the farmer to keep at his nurturing duties. This goes on into the second, third, fourth and even some part of the fifth year; when suddenly, the Chinese bamboo tree shoots between eighty to ninety solid feet high in the air, in just six weeks.

Give that a good thought. Did the growth really occur in six weeks? I bet you don't think it does. It took five years of labour without visible results to produce "sudden" growth within six weeks.

WHAT IF THE FARMER GAVE UP?

What if he sold the land, convinced that the seeds didn't germinate due to a curse cast on the land by his ancestors? I mean, if you've done all that is required of you and a land still doesn't yield her increase, won't you think something was wrong with the land?

What If the farmer felt something was wrong with his seeds? He would go purchase another from a different dealer, only to get the same results.

He will continue to move from one place to the other in search of a "better land". He would keep wasting money buying from different dealers only to be frustrated in the end because the growth of his bamboo is neither dependant on the land nor the seed dealer but in the process ordained by God for the bamboo.

HOW HAVE YOU TREATED YOUR CHINESE BAMBOO?

Your Chinese bamboo could be a dream, a vision, a ministry, a business or a simple instruction God laid in your heart. How long have you been nurturing it?

It seems normal to feel like something is wrong with the land where you've sown- the environment, the relationships you've invested in, the policies guiding the sector.

It seems normal to think something is wrong with your seeds- my calling isn't the reigning one, nobody accepts it, others don't understand it, no popular person has endorsed me yet.

It seems normal to question your abilities – I'm not applying the manure properly, I'm not trained enough, I'm not knowledgeable enough, I'm not certified yet.

While these thoughts seem normal in the face of empty barns, it is abnormal to abandon your dream, vision, assignment, mandate, business, ministry or what have you because you think any of the above "normal" thoughts.

The next time you are tempted to switch base, trade your calling for another person's or abandon your vision, remember that great rewards take long to arrive while outstanding rewards take longer to arrive. You can have your great reward today and pass on your outstanding reward, or wait today for your outstanding reward and pass on the great reward.

Beyond choice, the one quality that determines if people pass on great rewards and go on till outstanding reward arrives, is consistency.

WHAT IS CONSISTENCY?

To be consistent is to act the same way or do something overtime. Consistency is therefore the quality or condition of being consistent (Collins Dictionary).

I believe that consistency is the degree of firmness in character. It refers to harmony between one's thoughts, speeches, beliefs and actions.

Consistency is a character issue and Like most character issue it can only be imbibed through practice.

DYNAMICS OF CONSISTENCY

Many people decide to be consistent every new year but they soon slack back into their old ways because they don't understand the dynamics of consistency. The word dynamics refers to the forces or properties which stimulate growth and development within a system or process. Hence, we are looking at **the forces that stimulate the development of consistency in character.** These forces are Prize, Drive and Price (PDP).

The force of prize

Prize is the thing given as a reward to the winner of a competition or in recognition of an outstanding achievement.

You can't gain mastery in consistency when you don't even know why you have to do what you have to do.

The prize is your why. You should ask, Why did the Lord call me? Why did He instruct me to start that business? Why did He send me to children with disabilities?

When you identify why, you will readily commit to the course in the face of drought, delay or distress.

While it's up to you to decide your prize, I have one advice for you on that-**Never make anything ephemeral your prize.**

Ephemeral things are temporal. They end in this life time. They include money, fame, awards, recognition, accolades, privileges and various material possessions. While those are good source of motivation in other areas of life, they will fail you in ministry. If you must gain mastery over consistency in ministry, your prize must be something eternal.

I have had moments when I didn't feel like hosting any of those conferences we host annually at the Birthplace Empowerment Foundation but in times like that, I often remember my why.

My Prize is not so much in the many lives that these conferences equip as much as it is in getting this one remark from Jesus-"Annie, You finished". Those words from Him are my prize. I desperately want Him to say that to me when I'm done executing the mission on earth. Those words are the reason I will keep showing up in this mission no matter what storm rocks my boat. And oh, many storms have rocked my boat.

What is your Prize? What's the reason you started that business or ministry? Why are you on that lane? If your why isn't strong enough, you most likely would quit before your Chinese bamboo yields.

The force of drive

A drive is that which propels you towards a direction. You might want to call this your passion. Sadly, I know many passionate people who are grossly inconsistent. Are you one of those people who say they have passion for a cause, business or area of ministry and thirty years down the line with five children, a spouse, a car and a dog, they have nothing to show for their passion?

I don't totally agree when people say passion drives one. Passion only drives you when there is strength in your spirit.

The strength of your spirit man is determined by his temperature (cold, hot, lukewarm); the temperature of your spirit is determined by what you feed your soul with.

Passion is nothing but a strong desire. How strongly do you desire to see that thing God told you happen? If you strongly desire it, you will build strength in your spirit by protecting its temperature. You protect the temperature of your spirit by running a quality check on the information that enters your soul. You must ensure that the only information you allow is such that propels you towards the fulfillment of the assignment on your life.

Any information that dampens your spirit or squashes the possibility of the vision in your spirit must be avoided like a plague. The presence of negative information in your spirit leads to lukewarmness. If you are serious about being consistent on your assignment, you must guard against lukewarmness.

SUBTLE SIGNS OF LUKEWARMNESS

The problem with lukewarmness is that most people don't know when their sprit has slipped into that zone.

You know moments after a corporate or personal fast when you feel pumped up and power-stuffed, ready for anything on the Christian journey? Yeah right! Not until few weeks when you drag into the unexpected- tongues taste like soured milk, worship feels dry like pampers; personal bible study bores like calculus.

People often think that lukewarmness begins when prayer life and study life becomes a drag. If only we knew what and when the real problem begins. There is a huge difference between knowing something is wrong and knowing exactly what is wrong.

The Laodicea Church was a Christian community established in the ancient city of Laodicea now called Denizili in today's country known as TURKEY [1]. Jesus had this to say about them back then as written in Revelations 3:15-19 (NLT)

"I know all the things you do, that you are neither hot nor cold. I wish that you were one or the other! But since you are like lukewarm water, neither hot nor cold, I will spit you out of my mouth! You say, 'I am rich. I have everything I want. I don't need a thing!' And you don't realize that you are wretched and miserable and poor and blind and naked. So I advise you to buy gold from me—gold that has been purified by fire. Then you will be rich. Also buy white garments from me so you will not be shamed by your nakedness and ointment for your eyes

so you will be able to see. I correct and discipline everyone I love. So be diligent and turn from your indifference."

A closer look at the above verses reveals three subtle signs of lukewarmness.

1. Illusion
2. Indifference
3. Slothfulness

Illusion: This refers to something that deceives by producing a false or misleading impression of reality[2].

This people believed they were rich, had everything and didn't need anything. Meanwhile they were ***wretched, miserable ,poor, blind and naked.***

Isn't that how we sometimes feel we are doing okay because we still speak in tongues, read our bibles, pray and see answers, don't miss services, pay our tithe and all the routine we judiciously hang on to?

Don't get me wrong. These things are very important and I do them too but they aren't actual proofs that a Christian is hot! (We will get to the real deal soon).

The Laodicea church had all the routines in place and who knows, their church services were probably laced with people crying during worship in heavily goose-bumps-inspiring ambience, classy protocol team and all.

These things are enough to make any Christian/church feel they are doing okay.

Are you actually doing okay?

Indifference: This refers to lack of interest or concern[3]. One would wonder how indifference is an issue here.

You know how we can be so engrossed in our already pre-planned agenda that it becomes impossible to embrace the new? Times when we stick with our old plans, old methods of serving in the kingdom or sticking with a particular area or aspect that we don't care anymore when God is whispering a new agenda in our hearts.

For example, a church might be used to serving widows every month and God lays it on the heart of the leaders that He wants them to reach farmers in the community. Now, they bring it up on the board meeting and analyze to the point of paralysis, raising reasons upon reasons why they must stick with the ancient program. You hear things like, "that's how we've been doing it", "ministering to widows is still ministry; we don't have to do everything". That right there is indifference!

Let me drive this point home a bit. Assume I'm married to you and you say, "Sweet, I like apples". I note your preference and I get you apples consistently and after fifteen years in our marriage, you say, "Sweet, I like watermelons". Now you've told me your **"present"** preference but I continue to buy you apples just because you preferred them in the past. You tell me again and I say, "well honey, apples and watermelons are both fruits, they do the same thing. You've always liked apples after all".
Would you be happy with me? I bet that will hurt. You will definitely feel I'm not paying attention to your needs.

That right there is being indifferent.

What are those areas in your life that the Holy spirit has been saying, "honey I need you to make an adjustment here" but you've explained it away saying. "It's not a sin after all, I pay my tithe after all, I go to church after all, I sing worship songs to you after all"!

Are you still sure you're doing okay?

Slothfulness: This refers to being sluggardly, indolent or lazy[3]. I did justice to this subject in my book 7 Signs you are sabotaging your life. I will just speak about it here from a different perspective.

Ever tried to use a blunt knife to cut vegetables? (Rolling my eyes). That's my worse kitchen ordeal right there. The problem with blunt objects is ineffectiveness. They can't cut right and require extra effort that they don't reproduce on the job!

When something or someone is ineffective, they are unreliable, unproductive and are a waste of effort. Are you one of those who spend all your time speaking in tongues, reading your bible but you are chief procrastinator on the assignments that God gives you daily?

You are probably "prayerful" but the moment the Holy Spirit says, "Child, pray for this person", prayer suddenly feels like a drag.

Most people are only fervent in prayer when asking about their personal needs. When it's about souls or anything God is concerned about, they pray like God needed to beg them. Watch our churches. Haven't you noticed the zeal with which people pray against "witches from the village"? Head banging almost to a fall off, eyes shut till it's almost red, voices raised to the maximum; but as soon as the prayer point becomes "let's pray for missionaries in the northern states", voices becomes whispers, eyes open like angels tapped them. It is this kind of slack towards what really matters to God that made Him call the Laodicea church lukewarm!

The issue with lukewarm tea isn't that it isn't Liquid. It's still liquid. Like the Laodicea church, they were still "born again". However, the inconsistency in result/effectiveness was God's issue with them and with most of us today.

Hot water tea can warm up your chest in a cold season; cold water tea can make you come alive in a hot season. What purpose would a lukewarm tea serve other than make you want to puke/throw up?

When God has a pressing need over nations can He trust you? When a soul is running out of time and needs the love of Jesus can God send you? If God can't bank on you to deliver on assignments, then you are LUKEWARM no matter how high sounding your tongues might be.

FEATURES OF LUKEWARMNESS

Noticed how the Lord described the Lukewarm? *"You don't realize that you are **wretched** and **miserable** and **poor** and **blind** and **naked.** See what these descriptions really mean

<u>Wretched:</u>

Wretchedness is translated talaipóros in Greek. It means "beaten-down) from continued strain, leaving a person literally full of *callouses"*. Callouses is translated pórósis in Greek and means hardness of heart [3].

Therefore in plain English, Lukewarmness is a state in which we feel "tired" of the demands of our commitment to God and eventually become hardened. This explains why God says he wants us to pray for someone and we say, "well God I already covered them in the general prayer." God says start a children outreach we say, "I already teach children Sunday school at church.

We give such excuses believing God understands. We don't often see it is because we are strained from the pressures of service and haven't refueled. When you begin to give excuses for not obeying God swiftly and accurately, You are definitely beaten down by the strains of life and are working in hardness of heart. The bad thing is the illusion of lukewarmness wouldn't let one see this in time.

<u>Miserable</u>**:**

The word miserable is translated *eleeinos* in Greek. It means pitiful, in desperate need of mercy.[4]

The lukewarm think they have done so much for God and are in the position to offer so-called expert counsel to others. When they see someone else who is vibrant, eager and fervent (usually a new/young converts); they say things like "oh give him/her some time. She/he would soon learn that it's not by much zeal".

The lukewarm does not realize that the vibrancy, eagerness and fervency of the young convert are products of first love which they have lost!

God says, while they think they are okay, they are actually pitiful.

Poor:

This one strikes me like a grenade. It is translated pto-khos' in Greek and means one is deeply destitute, completely lacking resources. It is at this point I realized that poverty is in levels.

For instance, Mr Okon lives in a one room apartment with his seven children and wife in a ghetto somewhere. He is a motorcycle (okada) rider. Mr Okon who can afford some basic things is poor.

On the other hand, Mr. Dapo has no home, lives under the bridge, has neither education nor skill to earn a living. He has to depend on others for survival. Mr. Dapo who has no source of livelihood and can't help himself is destitute.

God says, Lukewarm Christians are like Mr Dapo (destitute). This is because they often lack the necessary resources to execute kingdom agenda. They've lost sensitivity, passion, zeal, faith and most times their joy. The problem again, is in this state we still think we are doing okay.

 Blind:

The word blind means one is deprived of understanding, judgment, or perception.[5]

If you ask me, this is both the root and stronghold of

lukewarmness. Blind people can't see their true state. Lukewarm Christians argue a lot with God, his principles and other Christians. They often can't perceive when a conversation is unnecessary. When they argue with God, they think that there is still much time. They don't see that the present/current instruction is the most crucial on the father's agenda.

<u>Naked:</u>

(Hands on my face) I don't want to see anyone's private property please. (Laughing out loudly)
Lukewarmness strips you off your garment of righteousness. Leaving you exposed to the enemy's ridicule
"Look, I will come as unexpectedly as a thief! Blessed is all who are watching for me, who keep their clothing ready so they will not have to walk around naked and ashamed." Revelation 16:15
You will never be consistent on your assignment if your spirit is lukewarm.

THE CURE FOR LUKEWARMNESS

"I know all the things you do, that you are neither hot nor cold. I wish that you were one or the other! But since you are like lukewarm water, neither hot nor cold, I will spit you out of my mouth! You say, 'I am rich. I have everything I want. I don't need a thing!' And you don't realize that you are wretched and miserable and poor and blind and naked.
So I advise you to buy gold from me—gold that has been

purified by fire. Then you will be rich. Also buy white garments from me so you will not be shamed by your nakedness and ointment for your eyes so you will be able to see. I correct and discipline everyone I love. So be diligent and turn from your indifference." Revelations 3:15-19 (NLT)

<u>Gold:</u>

Earlier we saw that lukewarm people are destitute, poor and miserable. They might have billions of dollars in their bank accounts, the best social connections and might have built the most successful businesses. However, these achievements aren't a picture of their true state- poverty/destitution/misery.

The Gold recommended here refers to the **true riches** of the kingdom of God. In Ephesians 3:8, Apostle Paul called it the unsearchable riches meaning it is unfathomable, abundant and massive wealth!

This wealth is incorruptible (cannot be destroyed, falsified nor forged). It's been tested, tried through the fire and certified as genuine. Some of the features of this gold/riches/wealth are

Riches of wisdom and knowledge

> Colossians 2:2b-3 *"... and of Christ in whom are hid all the treasures of wisdom and knowledge."*

Riches of grace

Ephesians 1:7, *"By whom we have redemption through his blood, the forgiveness of sins, according to the riches of his grace."*

Riches of God's glory

Ephesians. 1:18, *"That you may know what the hope of his calling is, and what is the **riches of the glory** of his inheritance in the saints."*

Ephesians 3:16, *"That he would grant unto you, according to the riches of his glory, to be strengthened with might by his Spirit in the inner man"*

Philippians 4:19, *"But my God shall supply all your need, according to his riches in glory by Jesus Christ."*

Remember Mathew 6: 9? Lay not up for yourselves treasures upon *earth, where moth and rust doth corrupt, and where thieves break through and steal (KJV)*

WHY GOLD?

Jesus recommended this because the true riches of the Kingdom cannot be got through self reliance. We must depend on the finished work of Christ and consistently walk in His will to obtain that which has been released unto us.

Salve:

Eye Salve was a Phrygian powder mentioned by Galen, for

which the medical school of Laodicea seems to have been famous[1]

The instruction Jesus gave was *" anoint thine eyes with eyesalve, that thou mayest see."(KJV)*. The word anoint is translated egchrió (eng-khree'-o)) in Greek which means to "rub in." [2] Hold that right there let's zoom in on the word eye salve. The word salve is translated kollourion (kol-loo'-ree-on) which means coarse bread[3]

Now we know that the word of God is JESUS (John 1:1) and JESUS is referred to as the bread of life (John 6:35). Therefore, Jesus was saying, rub me into your eyes so you can see clearly. Jesus is the foundation of true vision. Our vision becomes warped when we take our eyes of Him.

Lukewarmness is a tango dance with distraction and the only way to have our vision restored is to fix our eyes on the word/Jesus. What's your focus? The word or the world?

<u>White garments:</u>

This garment isn't some fancy handmade, Italian gown or robe. It is the garment of salvation, the robe of righteousness (Isaiah 61:10). A garment whose price tag is the blood of Christ. Jesus said get it from me because it is not available anywhere else.

We can never stand perfect or acceptable before God without this garment that comes only from JESUS.

Even though the Laodicea church was a group of "believers," they were naked because they had begun to feel comfortable and rely on their efforts.

This is a tricky situation for present day believers. Have you begun to walk in self righteousness? Ask the Lord to restore the garment of righteousness upon you. It is with this garment that we will partake in the wedding ceremony with the Lord and as His bride, we cannot afford to be ashamed or naked at His appearance. Read *Revelation 19:6-9*

Get lukewarmness off your spirit and watch your drive for the assignment on your life, sky rocket.

The force of price

Price is the worth of something. You can only commit to what costs you. Consistency becomes an auto response to the one who knows what a mission or vision costs him/her.

What have you sacrificed so far on your mission? What have you given up so far? That should spur you to show up consistently at your assigned post; and though we pay these prices, we still must bear in mind that the biggest price for every assignment is the blood of Christ.

Every time I have had to host a conference or an outreach and the bill scares me, I don't only think about God's ability to provide. I also think about the weight of Jesus' sacrifice for the lives He wishes to reach through me.

You are inconsistent with the assignment because you haven't realized the price yet. It costed Christ His life. Stop going on and off your duty post.

If you would master the dynamics of Prize (Your eternal why), Drive (A fervent Spirit birthed desire), Price (making sacrifices for your mission), inconsistency will be sent on exile from your life.

FIVE AREAS YOU NEED TO DEVELOP CONSISTENCY

Being a character issue, consistency reflects in every area of your life. If you build it in one area, you will find yourself consistent in other areas of your life. Below are five important areas where you need to commit to developing consistency.

Consistency in Association

The undoing of most people God sends on grand missions is sentiments. When you start becoming overly conscious about what people around will say should you uphold biblical principles, you will most likely end up living a double standard life.

People are not supposed to be comfortable doing wrong around you. There should be something about you that makes others respect your presence so much that they avoid evil when you happen to be in their midst.

Don't be someone who switches from saved to sinner when your environment changes. To ensure you don't become such a person, you must be intentional about your association. While you will forever relate with the unsaved so long as you are on earth, you must ensure that your close and consistent association is made up of people who uphold same principles and values as you. You also must ensure that you have absolutely nothing to do with the occult or cults. *"You can't drink from the cup of the Lord and demons"* 1Corinthians 10:21. If you miss out on consistency in association, you won't' last on the mission.

Henceforth, evaluate your associations regularly in order to ensure that they are godly and beneficial to you and the mission.

Consistency in Surrenderance:

Who do you submit to? The Lord or your ambitions? His word or your cravings? No one can serve two masters- Luke 16:13.

Consistently practice submitting to Christ and His will for your life. You must intentionally demonstrate loyalty to God and His principles. When you have to choose, eliminate the options that poses a hindrance to the mission God has assigned to you. Don't let Jesus be Lord on Sunday morning and disregard Him on Monday morning. Surrender consistently.

Consistency in Service

You are going to have many days when you would feel like quitting. You might even have valid reasons on some of those days but pause for a moment on days like that and think on 1 Corinthians 15:58 and get back to work.

"Therefore my dear and brothers and sisters, stand firm. Let nothing move you. Always give yourselves fully to the work of the Lord, because you know that your labour in the Lord is not in vain." (NIV)

The Chinese bamboo farmer doesn't see results in the first , second, third or fourth year. If he stopped caring for the spot where the seed was planted, the seeds would grow but they may not grow to their maximum capacity of ninety feet. Therefore just as Galatians 6:9 tells us, *"Let us not become weary in doing good for at the proper time we will reap a harvest if we do not give up." NIV)*

There is a due time for the reward to show up. The reward is certain. You only need to decide if you want to wait for the full reward by consistently serving on your mission or get nothing or a tampered result by abandoning your mission.

Consistency in intimacy with God:

1 John 2:27 says, *"You have received the Holy spirit and He lives within you, so you don't need anyone to teach you what is true. For the spirit teaches you everything you need to know and what he teaches is true. It is not a lie. So just as he has taught you, remain in fellowship with Christ." (NLT)*

How can the Lord teach you when you don't even have his time? Your prayer life is epileptic, your study life is epileptic, you obedience is epileptic and you expect to excel on the mission? Fix that right now darling, fix that right now!

Consistency in speech:

It's a terrible thing when no one can trust your words. Mathew 5:37 says, *"Let your yes be yes and your no, be no.*

Consistency in speech entails that you keep your word. When you say something is red and they ask you next year, don't say it is maroon just because you want to get something or protect something. When you say you are going to do something, get it done.

 If you built consistency in these five areas of your life, it will reflect powerfully on your life, marriage, business and ministry.

11

THE POWER OF HABIT

Wining is habit. Unfortunately, so is losing- Vince Lombardi

A father's request

A rich man once asked an old, wise man to help his son change his bad habits. The old man asked his son to take a walk with him through the garden. After taking a few steps, the wise man stopped and asked the young man to pluck a small flower out of the ground. The young man grabbed the plant with his fingers and easily plucked it out. The wise man nodded and they resumed walking.

A few seconds later, they stopped again and the wise man pointed towards another plant, a bit larger than the last. The young man grabbed it with his hand and plucked it out of the ground with a bit of effort.

"Now pluck out that one" the wise man said pointing towards a bush. The young man grabbed the bush with both of his hands and using all of his strength, barely managed to pluck it out of the ground.

"Now you see that small tree, there? Try and pluck that one." The young man grabbed the trunk with both hands, pulled as hard as he could but he couldn't even move it.

"It's impossible master. I can't do it."

"You see my boy, it's the same with our habits. If we let them grow and take root it becomes harder and harder for us to stop them."[1]

HOW HABITS ARE FORMED

Habit is an acquired mode of behavior that has become nearly or completely involuntary. **It is** a settled tendency or usual manner of behaviour.[2]

The *American Journal of Psychology* defines "habit as a fixed way of thinking, willing, or feeling acquired through **previous repetition** of a mental experience. The word repetition is the pillar of habit formation.

However, there are three psychological patterns (habit loop) that influence repetition which in turn leads to the formation of a habit. They are- the cue, the behavior, and the reward.

<u>The cue</u> is the thing that causes the habit to come about. It is the trigger of the habitual behavior. It is that thing that tells our brains to go into automatic mode and let a behavior occur. This could be anything that one's mind associates with that. For example, drinking alcohol can trigger/cue the desire to smoke. Waking up can trigger/cue a desire to pray, watch TV, text the love of your life, take coffee; all depending on previous repetition.

<u>The behavior</u> is the actual habit or routine that one exhibits. A behaviour is said to have occurred when one does the specific action required by the cue or trigger. Using our previous examples, the actual behaviour would be smoking after drinking alchohol, praying once you wake up or texting the love of your life.

<u>The reward</u> is a positive feeling one gets from the behaviour. Still on our previous examples, the reward for smoking could be calmed nerves, feelings of being high, feelings of warmth. The reward for calling a loved one first thing after you awake could be feelings of being loved, feelings of being held warmly. All these feelings are interpreted as positive by the brain.

Do you understand?

This positive feeling is therefore stored and resurfaces the next time we are faced with that cue or trigger. The next time, a smoker takes alcohol (the cue), his brain reminds him of the pleasure/good feeling he derived from smoking the last time. He therefore gives into the craving (behaviour) and experiences the good feeling (reward). This is why it is called a **habit loop**.

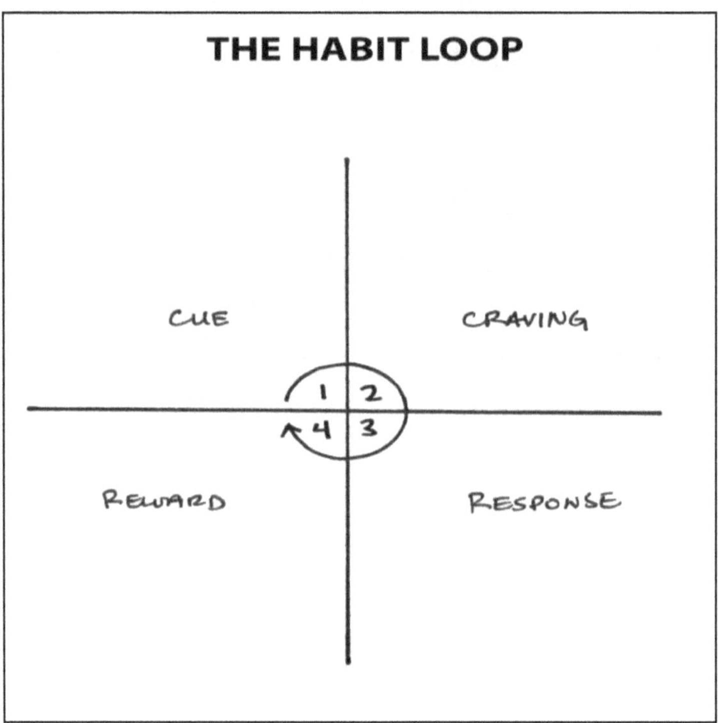

Fig 1: This representation of the habit loop is a combination of language that was popularized by Charles Duhigg's book-The Power of Habit, and a design that was popularized by Nir Eyal's book-Hooked.

WHY HABITS ARE A BIG DEAL

About 40% to 45% of what we do every day feels like a decision, but it's actually habit.[5]

See this, "Neuroscientists have traced our habit-making behaviors to a part of the brain called the basal ganglia, which also plays a key role in the development of emotions, memories and pattern recognition.

Decisions, meanwhile, are made in a different part of the brain called the prefrontal cortex. But as soon as a behavior becomes automatic, the decision-making part of your brain goes into a sleep mode of sorts.

"In fact, the brain starts working less and less," says Duhigg. "The brain can almost completely shut down. And this is a real advantage, because it means you have all of this mental activity you can devote to something else."

That's why it's easy while driving or parallel parking to completely focus on something else: like the radio, or a conversation you're having.

"You can do these complex behaviors without being mentally aware of it at all," he says. "And that's because of the capacity of our basal ganglia: to take a behavior and turn it into an automatic routine." [4]

Habits can be extremely useful and it would be impossible to run our lives without them. They automate many of the routine activities in our lives and free up our minds so that we are capable of concentrating on higher level activities.

For instance, if we had to consciously think about basic functions like walking or chewing our food or talking, we would have no mental ability available to perform other functions. The ability to write or type automatically allows us to focus on producing a great article, letter, email or novel. Similarly, walking by automatic processes allows us to be able to think about where we are going! We have thousands of these good 'habits' that our muscle memory has built up over time. Even breathing can be thought of a deeply ingrained habit. Driving a car and riding a bike are all a series of habits and actions we perform without conscious intent. Therefore, habits play an important role in simplifying our lives and REDUCING the amount of sensory stimuli we need to process.

It's estimated that out of every 11,000 signals we receive from our senses, our brain only consciously processes 40. Habits save us energy as by their nature they are automatic and require little physical and mental strength, for instance brushing your teeth or tying your shoelaces require very little mental energy.

Good habits serve to create routine, order and efficiency. Unfortunately bad habits have the opposite effect and can lock us into negative or rigid patterns of behaviour. Bad habits such as overeating, smoking or driving too fast can be damaging to our health and wellbeing.

Our brains are very powerful and are constantly scanning for patterns in our lives or things it can turn into habits. Unfortunately, our subconscious mind does not discriminate between good and bad habits and anything that is repeated over time has the potential to become a habit.

Fortunately, we can take control of this process and CONSCIOUSLY CHOOSE which thoughts, actions and behaviours will become habits.[6]

HELP, I HAVE POOR HABITS!

Habits influence your life. Habits determine if you win or lose in both the little and big things that matter to you. Habits can make or mar goals. They largely influence the possibility of your wishes becoming wins and ultimately determine if you fulfill your assignment at the end of your stay on earth.

So how do you deal with those poor habits that are preventing you from living fulfilled?

The first thing you need to do is to
Identify those poor habits

Now take a paper and pen and write out those habits that you know are preventing you from effectively leading the great life you were designed and created to live.

<u>It will help a great deal if you grouped them into the **seven dimensions of life**</u> as seen below

Spiritual dimension refers to your relationship with God.

Social dimension refers to your relationship with people such as family, colleagues, strangers, neighbors, friends, dates.

Mental dimension refers to your mind which encapsulates your thoughts and beliefs

Career dimension refers to the occupation you have chosen to do for a significant period of your life.

Financial dimension refers to all your money related actions such as earning, saving, spending and investing.

Physical dimension refers to your body and state of its health.

Ministerial dimension refers to everything surrounding your purpose, calling and assignment on earth.

It is important to note at this point, that you cannot stop a habit abruptly. You simply **replace** poor, old habits with better, new habits. Hence, you can't wake up and quit smoking if you've been smoking every morning for thirty years. Abruptly stopping isn't going to work. You will eventually have a relapse and it will be fatal. The same goes for habits such as perpetually masturbating, drinking coke or any other addictive behaviour you may have identified.

The key to replacing poor old habits with new ones, is to
Identify the triggers/cues

Earlier we saw that it is the cue/trigger and the reward that really determine why a habit occurs not the behaviour itself. Therefore to undo poor habits, we must first identify the triggers responsible for each bahaviour you have listed.

For instance, if your poor habit under finances was impulsive spending, a close observation may reveal the trigger to be sadness. Therefore when you are sad (cue/trigger), you crave happiness (craving) which leads you to spend impulsively (habit) after which you feel happy (reward).

HOW TRIGGERS WORK

As taught by Charles Duhigg, Habits are triggered or cued in five primary ways- Time, location, preceding event, emotional state and people.

Trigger 1: **Time**

Time triggered behaviours include brushing your mouth when you wake up in the morning, saying the Angelus prayer at 12pm (If you are catholic), checking your emails as soon as you wake up.

A close observation to your daily living will show that you mindlessly repeat some tasks/actions same time every day. Those action/tasks are examples of time based triggers/cues.

How to use time-based triggers/cues to form a desirable habit

Fix a time and decide on what action to take during that time and stick to the schedule.

Before long, you will be mindlessly doing that same time every day.

Some years ago while at the university, I wanted to form the habit of waking up to pray at 5am. I set my alarm to wake me up at 5 am and as soon as I wake, I leave my hostel to a private place to pray. Over ten years after, I no longer use an alarm. I automatically awake at 5 am. It's up to me decide if I want to go out and pray or pray in bed but I definitely wake up.

You can form healthy habits too using time-based triggers.

Trigger 2: **Location**

Location-based triggers/cue is those that influence you to do something based on the environment. For example, you might notice that you pray well (with more concentration and for a longer time) only when you are in church. Perhaps you tend to focus more on God when you see an image of the cross hanging on the church altar or as a result of the music sang in church.

Praying well in this case is clearly as a result of your environment or location-based cue.

Another example is when you drink because you and your friends are hanging out in a bar and they are all drinking.

How to use location-based triggers/cues to form a desirable habit

Several research studies by David Neal and Wendy Wood from Duke University have discovered that new habits are actually easier to perform in new locations. One theory is that we mentally assign habits to a particular location. This means that all of the current places that you're familiar with (your home, your office) already have behaviors, habits, and routines assigned to them. **If you want to build new habits in these familiar locations, then you need to overcome the cues that your brain has already assigned to that area.** Meanwhile, building a new habit in a new location is like having a blank slate. You don't have to overcome any pre-existing triggers.[7]

Using our example of prayer above, church shouldn't be the only place where you pray well. Therefore to improve how well you pray at home, you can introduce elements of your church environment into your home. You could affix a cross in your bedroom or if it is the music in church that helps you pray well, play the music in your home and after a while the habit of concentrating and praying longer in your home (new location) is formed.

Trigger 3: **Preceding event**

This refers to cues/triggers prompted as a result of something that happened earlier. Some habits are as a response or result of something else that normally happen in your day to day life.

For instance, in secondary school the ring of bell at break time precedes consumption of soft drink and snacks. That's also when you probably hangout with your close friend in other arm of the same class as you; that's when you use the rest room.

How to use preceding event-based triggers/cues to form a desirable habit

Choose a preceding event and decide on an accompanying habit which you intend to replace the old, poor habit and simply **do** the preferable habit after the preceding event. Forming or replacing habits is totally dependent on repetition of an action. Therefore DO what you have decided to do after the preceding event. The key word to getting result is **doing.**

Trigger 4: **Emotional state**

Some people binge when they are sad. Others masturbate when they are stressed. Another group of people self inflict pain when they grieve. Many poor habits such as these and others like impulsive spending, excessive sleeping, incessant clubbing are often results of our emotional state.

How to use Emotional state-based triggers/cues to form a desirable habit

Assuming you identified masturbation as a habit you will like to replace, you will need to observe when you masturbate. You may notice it happens when you are stressed. Stress is the preceding event based trigger in this case. The reason you automatically default to the act when stressed is because your brain and body craves the feel good hormone (Oxytocin) released after an orgasm/climax (the reward). Oxytocin reduces stress level and leads to relaxation and sleepiness.

To avoid masturbating when stressed, you need to engage in an activity that gives you the same level of relaxation as the behaviour/ routine (masturbation). **Examples of behaviours that trigger the release of Oxytocin and can effectively replace masturbation are**

- Professional massage or you can hop on a massage machine.
- Give a gift to someone you know would really appreciate it. Soak in their positive reaction.
- Share a meal with someone you really care about and who cares about you in return.
- Soak in a hot tub.
- Burn essential oil candles such as lavender, rose, ylang ylang, frankincense.

- Chat with someone you care about and who cares about you too.
- Pet a dog or cat or anything you consider a pet. I prefer dogs to cat because I notice they know how to receive and give love so long as you are familiar with them.
- Hug people when you greet them.
- Have a time out with father (The Lord) in an atmosphere of pure love and worship (works for me every time).
- Cry if you feel so.

Trigger 5: **People**

Jim Rohn a very successful American entrepreneur, author and motivational speaker who passed on in 2009 said, "You are the average of the five people you spend the most time with."

People can trigger behaviours in you that you normally wouldn't exhibit. This is why you crave a drink when you hang out in a bar with friends who drink. You crave a more intimate relationship with God when you hang out with people who effortlessly demonstrate intimacy with God.

How to use People-based triggers/cues to form a desirable habit

Surround yourself with people who have the habits you desire to cultivate and do as they do.

Now that you know how triggers work and can identify the

triggers associated with your old. Poor habits, you should

Choose a trigger/cue

Would you want to create a time bound cue for your new habit or a location based one? Would you rather choose a people based trigger or an emotional state trigger/cue? Whichever trigger/cue you pick is up to you. **The key to choosing a successful cue is to pick a trigger that is very specific and immediately actionable**

For Instance, If you want to build a new habit of scheduling your daily activities, you could start by choosing a time-based cue which goes,

"Every night before I go to bed I will list out what I am to do the next day." While this might work, it is not specific.

A more specific trigger/cue would be, "Every night at 7pm or just after dinner, I will write out a list of what to do the next day on my green diary." This isn't only specific it is also immediately actionable.

5 SIMPLE HABITS THAT MAKE A MORE FULFILING LIFE

Fulfillment !

That word evokes different meaning to each one of us. Whether it means grabbing that promotion you've eyed for years, shopping in Dubai with a loved one, marrying the bae or boo of your dreams or finally getting to start that ministry or pet project you've harboured for years? These simple actions are sure to bring you to that point where you scream "alas!" on fulfillment board.

<u>Define:</u> Knowing exactly what you want is pivotal to gaining or losing fulfillment in life. Take out time to clearly state what you want out of every aspect of your God-blessed life. From career, to relationships, to ministry and health, have a clear statement on what you want out of life.

<u>Follow:</u> It's one thing to know exactly what you want and another to take the route leading to it. Follow through with your plans/ strategies. Never allow any obstacle keep you on the ground for too long. You heard that? F-O-L-L-O-W. Quitters never experience fulfillment in anything!

<u>Re-evaluate:</u> I know how okay it feels to keep doing something just because it has been working through the years. You never will know how awesome feels until you add awe to some. Re-evaluate your actions, your goals, your decisions, your best practices over time and you will find an awe to add to the some you thought was great all the while.

<u>Assert:</u> To assert is state a fact or belief confidently and forcefully. This doesn't make you a neurotic fissure (don't check that up by the way, Laughs).
It helps you produce results in line with your conviction. You believe you are amazing right? You believe that those goals of yours can be achieved don't you? Now when it looks like they won't come from paper to present, state aloud what you believe will happen to you.

Ever seen proverbs 12: 14? *"**From the fruit of their lips people are filled with good things** and the work of their hands brings them reward."(NIV-emphasis added).*
So while you work towards it, confess your convictions!

<u>Enjoy:</u> Okay now honey, how about the little successes of everyday life? Celebrate them. Personally, each time I get my hair done, I admire myself in the mirror and sing my beauty to my hearing.

So you wrote one paper out of ten required to become certified, enjoy the feeling of triumph that the moment provides.

Did you just speak to someone about Jesus and they gave their lives to Christ but didn't show up on Sunday, still enjoy the moment of salvation and go back for them later.
ENJOY, ENJOY, ENJOY each moment on your way to the main deal.

12

THE POWER OF FLEXIBILITY

If you are truly flexible and go until... there is really very little you can't accomplish in your life time. Tony Robbins

My little world has broken

Once upon a time there was a spring who lived happily and safely inside a pen. Although he heard many noises coming from outside, he lived believing that outside his world inside the pen, there was nothing good. Even just to think about leaving his pen made him so scared that he was quite content to spend his life compacting and stretching himself again and again inside that tiny space.

One day, the ink ran out, and when the pen's owner was

busy changing it, there was an accident. The spring was flung through the air and landed in the toilet drain, well out of sight. Terrified, and cursing his bad luck, the spring was flushed through pipe after pipe, each time thinking it might be his end. During the journey, he did not dare open his eyes out of deep fear. Nor did he stop crying. Swept away by the water, he travelled on and on and on, until he ended up in a river.

When the river current lost its force, and the spring could see that things had calmed down a bit, he stopped crying and listened all around him. Hearing birdsong and wind in the trees, he felt encouraged to finally open his eyes. What the spring saw was the pure, crystal waters of the river, the rich green rocks of the riverbed, and all kinds of fishes of, whose skin seemed to dance under the sunlight. Now he understood that the world was much greater than the space inside the pen, and that there had always been many things outside, waiting to be enjoyed.

After spending a while playing with the fishes, he went over to the riverbank, and then moved on to a field of flowers. There he heard weeping. He followed the sound, which took him to a lovely flower that had been flattened by a rabbit, and could no longer stand up straight. The spring realized that he could help the flower, so he offered to be his support. The flower accepted, and slipped through the middle of the spring. There they lived happily together. they laughed years later when remembering how the spring used to think that all there was to life was being a sad and fearful spring. [1]

Like the spring in the story, you may have had a time in life when you didn't think anything good could come out of a disaster. The fact that you are still here on earth and reading this book despite many unforeseen storms that hit you, is proof that storms are not the end of life.

Flexibility is adjusting to change with a good attitude.[2] While we may not have full control over what happens to us in life, we have full control over how we respond.

Inflexible people do not finish through on tasks, they abandon responsibilities and surrender to depression when plans don't go as imagined. If you must win at anything in life, If you must live out the fullness of your purpose and execute the mandate on your life, you must build this virtue of flexibility.

WHAT IT MEANS TO BE FLEXIBLE

Flexibility isn't the same as readily compromising on big things such as your faith, selling out your family, or betraying friends just because you want to survive a hit. It actually means

- Being wise enough to **anticipate change** and prepare accordingly.

LET'S LEARN FROM PALM TREES.

Palm trees survive heavy storms because they bend with the wind instead of breaking under the wind's pressure. They anticipate change in weather by growing in such a way that they can bend and not break. Unlike traditional trees, palm trees are not made of wood. "Instead, you'll find a jumble of spongy tissue, scattered instead of arranged" inside a palm. Most trees lay down rings as they grow every year but not the palm tree; some of its cells are malleable, and others can easily flex and then return to their original position.[3]

What are you built of? While things are rosy, are you developing your mind/soul, spirit and body to survive hits? It is wisdom to anticipate change and prepare for it. Prepare for changes in your relationship or marriage, prepare for changes in ministry, and prepare for changes in business. Prepare for changes in your body, you won't always be young and as strong as you are today.

One practical way to prepare or build up while anticipating change is to fund your retirement account, get an insurance plan, eat healthily in your youth, nurse an intimate relationship with God in good and bad times, invest time building valuable friendships with people because someday, a hurricane may just hit. You never know.

- Being humble enough to **adjust when you should**.

The palm tree has the reputation of being the world's most resourceful and useful plant. Everything from root to chaff is useful. This doesn't make the palm tree inflate with pride and stand tall in the face of strong winds. It understands that it needs to adjust with the wind. That is the reason it survives storms in which other trees break.

When faced with challenges lean back and figure out areas in which you need to adjust. You may need to cut back on data usage to save up for your house rent, you may need to go without buying new clothes for a whole year to pay up children's school fees. It doesn't make you less of a person. You are still you and humble enough to adjust to change in other to achieve a higher goal.

- Being observant enough **to see the good.**

Palm trees don't curse when the wind hits them. As they sway in the glory of a hurricane they see it as an opportunity to wave in adoration to God who made them flexible enough to survive hurricanes.

Train your eyes to intentionally see the good in a failed plan, a disappointment, a betrayal, a failed relationship, a surgery, a disease, a loss. The goodness in these experiences won't jump at you; you have to intentionally look for it.

What recent ugly experience was your chance to care freely wave to the Lord in adoration and gratitude (regardless) as the wind swayed you from left to right? Did you wave your praise or did you voice a curse?

- Being disciplined enough to **finish the job.**

Palm trees don't uproot themselves in frustration. They don't abandon their responsibility of bearing nuts for us just because a stern hurricane hit them mercilessly.

You must never abandon your purpose or God given assignments because life dealt you an ugly blow. By God's grace, I speak as one who like you, has had life's fierce fist hit her health, finances and emotions. Here I am, still standing, still serving, still writing in order to minister to you. Please do

the same for me and the billion others tied to your destiny. Don't let suicide have you, you have a job to finish. Don't let depression hold you bound, you have a job to finish. Don't let the cold of loneliness make you sniff out the glory of your calling prematurely because you have a job to finish.
Can I get an amen?

- Being upright enough to **do the right thing.**

Despite the pressure from the wind, the palm tree doesn't stay bowed. It rises upright to do what it should do - stand. Honey, I know you got hit by an ugly divorce. I know your parents abandoned you as a child. I know your boyfriend of ten years disappeared on you, I know you just found you had cancer, I know the doctor said you are infertile but please would you be upright enough to just do the right thing which is TO STAND?

Stand on God's word regardless of how torn you feel, stand on God's love regardless of how far below the belt life hits you. That's all you are required to do even when the future looks bleak. Just stand and courageously express the strength and dominion God unleashed in you before the world began.

HOW FLEXIBILITY INFLUENCES YOUR SUCCESS

<u>Flexibility prepares you for adversity:</u>
You are better equipped to handle tough times in life when you are flexible.

<u>Flexibility reduces your stress level:</u>

It makes you seek an alternate route to your goal instead of worrying yourself into frustration.

<u>Flexibility empowers you to finish:</u>

You will be able to accomplish projects regardless of what obstacle comes up.

<u>Flexibility improves your worth:</u>

Flexibility leads you in paths that spurs development and growth for you, thereby increasing your worth. You are never the same as when you first got hit by an adversity.

<u>Flexibility creates balance:</u>

Your life will be a chaos if you are trying to hold on to thoughts and methods that clearly aren't giving you the desirable results. While holding on to one area of your life, you may be losing the other. Being flexible enables you to intelligently incorporate other thoughts and methods in your routine for improved results.

13

THE POWER OF REWARD

Notice the small things. The rewards are inversely proportional- Liz Vassey

G.M Matheny, a former Navy diver and current Missionary in Romania shared the story below about the one time he made the honour roll in seventh grade.

The one time I made the Honour roll

The only time I made the honor roll was in the seventh grade. The reason I never did before or after is because I wasn't interested in it. If you say I should have been, you're right, but then I didn't care. All I wanted was just to get through school.

My older sister, on the other hand, always made the honor roll, and she loved to show Dad her report card. This usually got me into trouble because my report card came out at the same time as my sister's, and Dad would say, "Son, where is yours?" Then I had to find my report card and show him, while my sister stood behind and listened as I was rebuked.

What motivated me to make the honor roll, that one time in seventh grade, were two girls who had made fun of my grades. They had made the honor roll for the semester and were congratulating each other when I decided I would join the conversation. I said, "I could make the honor roll if I wanted. All you've got to do is study." They stopped and stared at me and then just laughed out loud and walked off! I thought, "They really think I'm stupid." I decided this once I would do my best and make the honor roll!

That next semester, on my first test I got a *B*, which really bothered me because I thought, with all the effort I put in, I would surely have earned an *A+*. Then a terrifying thought came over me: "Maybe I really can't do this!"

I'm glad on my second test I merited an *A*; otherwise, I might have given up. By the way, I had to move away from my friends and sit up front in class because my buddies would cut up, and I could not listen.

This brought me a little persecution. "You trying to be teacher's pet? You think you're better than we are, don't you?" Actually, it was "no" to both questions. I just wanted to make the honor roll.

When report cards came out, I already knew I would be on the honor roll because I had asked each teacher. My old friends had that sick look on their faces when they received their report cards, and I could not help but laugh; I knew that feeling well.

There were two things I did with my report card. First, I found those two girls who had laughed at me. I walked straight up to them and shoved my report card in their faces and said, "This is my report card!" They stared at my grades in disbelief, and then I laughed really loud and walked off. Second, I went home and waited for my dad, sitting outside on the front porch. My sister came home and wanted to know why I was waiting outside, and I said, "You'll find out."

When Dad arrived home, I put my report card in his face and said, "Look, Dad!"

He put down his lunch pail and began to read my grades and then said, "I'm proud of you son!" And added, "I guess you will be getting grades like this from now on?" I just shrugged my shoulders. What's the point?[1]

NO WISH IS OUT OF REACH

Matheny's story proves that no wish is out of reach if you are certain you want it, know why you want it and what is required for you to make it happen.

So far I have shown you how to clarify your desires, understand your wishes and turn them into wins. At this point I am going to show you how to harness the power of rewards in turning your wishes into wins.

HOW REWARD WORKS

A reward is the thing given in recognition of service, effort, or achievement.[2]

Think about the one time you were recognized for an effort or achievement. Perhaps you got a blue ribbon from your teacher, or your mum hugged you for washing the dishes or your spouse said thank you and finally bought you something you have been asking for because you pleased them.

How did you feel?

Rewards make us feel good about ourselves. We enjoy the feeling and long for a repeat. This longing for the good feeling can make us continue with the effort or achievement that brought about the reward.

However, it is not every reward that has the capacity to **continuously** spur you to continue with an effort or achievement. This is because the human soul is built in a way that the will to continue or sustain anything is fueled from within. That is why you may motivate someone to do something or be something and they do or become that thing but the moment you stop pushing, they default to what they really, really wished to do or become. For a reward to bring about sustainable motivation towards a desired outcome (wish),

The reward must be from within

For instance, you may consistently tell a child not to leave his shoes in the living room. The child keeps leaving his shoes in the living room and only remembers to take them in when he/she sees you approaching.

At some point, the child may just leave it there because he is unhappy with you and knows that he can ruin your mood by leaving his shoes in the living room. Therefore the back and forth between you both continues. But it gets different when you convince the child that he is organized, clean and diligent therefore leaving his shoes in the living room makes him disorganized, dirty, and lazy.

A child who doesn't want to either see himself or be seen in that negative light will adjust. The next time, he wants to drop his shoes in the living room, he will remember that he is organized, clean and diligent therefore his shoes shouldn't be found in the living room.

This internal reminder of who he is and his wish (to be seen in a positive and responsible light), will make him keep his shoes in the right place without been reminded. Actions that stem from internal motivations are more sustainable than those from external motivations.

The essence of that reward must be convincing

Why do we have honour rolls in schools? I guess it is to motivate students to stretch towards excellence.

The honour roll will work for those who care about excellent grades. Not every one cares about excellent grades. Some people just want to be educated, others simply want the certificate to prove they have been to school. They have more interesting desires than stacking A's against their names. Remember Matheny?

Matheny wasn't convinced about the essence of being on the honour roll. The one time he got that roll, he had one wish- **to prove** to the girls (who laughed at him) and his father that he wasn't dumb, that he knew what it took to be on the honour roll and that he could meet that requirement. Therefore, the moment he proved his point, the honour roll had served its purpose in Matheny's life. There was no reason strong enough to motivate him back on the honour roll because he wasn't convinced about the big deal surrounding excellent grades and honour rolls.

HOW TO MAKE REWARD WORK FOR YOU

Now that you understand how reward works, you can wield its power to manifest your desires. Here is how to so;

<u>Clarify your desire:</u> Everything begins with been sure about what you really want. I already taught you how to do so in chapter 6.

<u>Turn your why in to a statement</u>
Now that you are sure of what you really want, turn your why (which is the reason you want that desire) into a statement.
For instance, if the reason you wanted to build a house is to be called a Landlord? The corresponding statement would be, " I am a Landlord. If the reason you want to get a PHD is

so you can secure a lecturing appointment? The corresponding statement would be, "I am a lecturer".
Write that statement where you can see it often and be reminded to declare it. Remember what we talked about the laws of manifestation?
Next,

Make your wish the reward

Normally, you would reward yourself after you have achieved your goal or grasped your wish. For instance, you may buy yourself a car, if you made a certain amount of profit; or indulge yourself in some unusual way after you made it on Forbes 30 under 30.
This time, don't do that. I didn't say don't buy a car after you have made mad profit. I am saying, instead of making the car your reward, make your wish the reward.

Here is what I mean,

Assuming your wish or desire was to be the best sales representative at your company this year, rather than think of what you would do for yourself after you made it, think of the wish as your reward for living. Thinking this way, would convince your soul that, **You deserve** the good you desire and that **You will receive** the good you desire. This **conviction** will in turn **motivate you from within** to strategize and stretch towards the fulfillment of your desire.

GRAB GOLD

GRAB GOLD

The mental victory is worth as much as a gold medal
Cameron van der Burgh

I've learnt that winning isn't everything. It is more about the journey but at the end of the day, I just want to stand on the podium with the gold medal.
Hope Solo

Winning a gold medal means you are the best in the world at that time
Michelle Carter

Good, better, best. Never let it rest. 'Til your good is better and your better is best.
St. Jerome

Set your goals high and don't stop till you get there.
Bo Jackson

What you get by achieving your goals is not as important as what you become by achieving your goals.
Zig Ziglar

14

BE IMPERVIOUS

Knowledge and application of your Identity in Christ makes you impervious to the enemy's threat- Anne Atulaegwu

Nehemiah possessed excellent qualities that propelled his rise up the ranks in Persia where he and some of the Israelites were on exile. He was the cup-bearer to the Persian king, Artaxerxes; a very important position that gave Nehemiah confidential access to the king.

Hanani, Nehemiah's brother and some men came to visit

Nehemiah after their trip to Jerusalem. They told Nehemiah about the trouble, disgrace and sufferings going on in the province of Judah and Jerusalem. Jerusalem had been torn down; its gates had been destroyed by fire.

Nehemiah was deeply hurt by this news and he prayed earnestly to God for favour with the king. The next day, the king noticed Nehemiah was sad. It was surprising to the king, as Nehemiah had never come before the king sad. When the king asked what the matter was, Nehemiah reported the state of Judah and Jerusalem to the king and asked for permission to go rebuild his city. God had heard his prayer the previous night and the king was willing to assist Nehemiah.

The king gave him letters addressed to the governors of the provinces he will travel through, instructing them to allow Nehemiah and his people travel through safely. The king also gave him a letter to the minister of Agriculture, instructing him to provide timber for the rebuilding of Jerusalem. God had provided all that was required for the rebuilding of Jerusalem; the men of Judah were willing to rebuild the ruined city under Nehemiah's leadership. The plan was perfect but they had enemies.

Sanballat, Tobiah, and Geshem two Ammonite and one Arab official heard of Nehemiah's plans and were offended. They didn't want anyone to help Israel and they couldn't bear seeing the ruined city rebuilt.

Since Nehemiah already had the king's permission and approval, it was impossible for them to oppose Nehemiah's mission legally. They resulted in a common but powerful weapon called mockery.

__1__Sanballat was very angry when he learned that we were rebuilding the wall. He flew into a rage and mocked the Jews, __2__saying in front of his friends and the Samarian army officers, "What does this bunch of poor, feeble Jews think they're doing? Do they think they can build the wall in a single day by just offering a few sacrifices? Do they actually think they can make something of stones from a rubbish heap and charred ones at that?" __3__Tobiah the Ammonite, who was standing beside him, remarked, "That stone wall would collapse if even a fox walked along the top of it!"
Nehemiah 4:1-3 (NLT)

Mockery, ridicule and threats are common but powerful instruments the enemy deploys against men on a mission. Many have abandoned their God-given assignments because someone or a group of people ridiculed them. Many plans will never move from <u>Paper to Play Out</u>[TM] because their set men or women are afraid of mockery.

Many wishes and dreams will die in the crevices of cold hearts just because an enemy spoke against the carriers and their purposes. You don't want to be in such statistics, do you? Not everyone will believe in your vision, idea, dream or calling. Many will ridicule you rather than keep their opinion to themselves.

Here is one truth, those who ridicule you are either jealous or angry you will outshine them. They do so because they feel inferior to you and the vision. You weren't born to be on the same level of shine as anyone, so it is okay to shine in a class of your own.

You are going to hear people mock your vision; they are going to undermine your mission. Many would hate your guts, do and say anything imaginable to demoralize you.

How you handle these moments determine if you win or lose in life.

WHAT IT MEANS TO BE IMPERVIOUS

It means to be unaffected, untouched, immune, invulnerable, insusceptible, unmoved by something.[1]

You are going to hear people laugh at your vision. Family members and dear friends may ridicule you at the start. You may even hear voices in your head accusing and reminding you of the past in ways that demoralizes you. You must be impervious to mockery and threats if you intend to record major wins in life.

HOW TO BE IMPERVIOUS TO MOCKERY

Recognize the spirit: Mockery is a demonic influence over the minds of people. The enemy does it to abort beautiful beginnings. You may hear words like; who do you think you are? You are not good enough, who will listen to a failure like you? Who would buy from a "nobody" like you? When you begin to hear words like this in your head or through others, recognize the spirit of mockery.

Shield your mind: Your mind is the citadel of all your

results. If the enemy succeeds in convincing and intimidating you to quit, you will never see your wishes become wins.

Shielding your mind requires you to boldly declare what God says concerning you. The enemy called you a good for nothing, call yourself Mr./Miss/Mrs. worthy of love, deserving of wealth, good for success. Speak it till your mind is restored in the place of confidence. Don't ever allow the enemy to speak last. Always respond using God's promises to you. You already know words are powerful. Let your mind hear God's promises in your own voice!

Petition God: A petition is an Ernest request or plea urging an authority to do something about a cause[2]. Nehemiah's prayer below was a petition to God against the mockery of Sanballat and the other officials.

> *Then I prayed, "Hear us, our God, for we are being mocked. May their scoffing fall back on their own heads.* Nehemiah 4:4 (NLT)

Sanballat and his men intended to discourage Nehemiah and the team from building or committing to their mission. Whenever you sense a strong attack against the vision under your watch and the people God has given you to execute a mission, petition God concerning your cause. Remember this verse? *'Do not be anxious about anything, but in every situation, **by prayer and petition**, with thanksgiving, present your requests to God.* Philippians 4:6 (NIV)

Keep building: Nehemiah and His men didn't stop building. They didn't postpone the mission to a later date when their mockers would stop or decide to support them. People of purpose don't have time to wait on odds to favour them. They move on regardless. You must know that the enemy is after the manifestation of your wins. He is manipulating people to frustrate you so you can abandon your mission. Regardless of what they say, build anyway!

15

BE THOUGHTFUL

Always be thoughtful of others- Jackie Joyner-Kersee

Nehemiah and the men didn't only have Sanballat's ridicule to deal with. They also had a powerful enemy within. His name was discouragement. Discouragement made the men overwhelmed by the weight of the work and the enemy's threat.

Then the people of Judah began to complain, "The workers are getting tired, and there is so much rubble to be moved. We will never be able to build the wall by ourselves."
Meanwhile, our enemies were saying, "Before they know what's happening, we will swoop down on them and kill them and end their work." The Jews who lived near the enemy came and told us again and again, "They will come from all directions and attack us!" Nehemiah 4:10-12 (NLT)

WHAT IT MEANS TO BE THOUGHTFUL

Thoughtfulness is the quality of giving/making helpful anticipation of the needs and happiness of others[1].
In order to dispel discouragement, Nehemiah told the Jews to remember their sons and daughters as well as the God who empowered them.

Every vision God gives is designed to favour posterity. Therefore it is necessary for you to consider generations to come when making decisions.

Discouragement envelopes your heart when you focus on the enemy's voice and the weight of your responsibilities in business, ministry, relationship. Nothing drains energy faster than this cold grim emotion. Discouragement magnifies the down sides and blind folds your spirit from the reality of the power at work in and for you.

When discouragement attacks your vibe, fight for your gold by being thoughtful. Think carefully about how your decision to quit or stay the course will affect posterity. Think carefully about how your action or inaction will place or displace you on Zion's hall of fame. Think carefully on the impact your decision will have on the entire human race.

If Einstein had given up on his 1000th attempt at inventing the light bulb, we probably wouldn't be in a world of Incandescent lamps, Compact fluorescent lamps, Halogen lamps, Metal halide Lamps, Light Emitting Diode, Fluorescent tube, Neon lamps ,High intensity discharge lamps. Clearly, posterity depended on Einstein's 1001st attempt as these varieties only happened because Einstein came through for the human race. Would you please come through for us?

When you give careful thought to your decisions and consequent actions, you will find reasons to see your mission to the point of victory. Many fail because they stopped paying close attention to how their actions affect God and others.

Always ask these questions when the going gets tough,

How will my action affect the people God has called me to serve?

How will my choices empower me to help them?

Who else wouldn't emerge if I let the flood drown me?

16

BE INTREPID

To the brave belong all things- Motto of the Celts

After I looked things over, I stood up and said to the nobles, the officials and the rest of the people, "Don't be afraid of them. Remember the Lord, who is great and awesome, and fight for your families, your sons and your daughters, your wives and your homes." Nehemiah 4:14 (NIV)

The word intrepid is being resolutely fearless; dauntless[1].

The words "do not be afraid occurs 365 times in the bible. It seems God was serving us a plate of resolute fearlessness for each day in the year.

When Nehemiah told the nobles and officials to be intrepid, he wasn't just being a motivational speaker. He taught them how to switch from being afraid to being intrepid when he said, *"Remember the Lord, who is great and awesome".*

You will easily cower before oppositions when you do not constantly remind yourself about God's reputation. I urge you to remember the Lord, who is faithful and true, and go start and finish what He asked you to.

I already showed you how to deal with fear and anxiety in earlier chapters. Get to work. Fix your mind on the God who sent you and fight for your gold!

Meet Intrepid David

Intrepid David has had his fair share of mockery by his elder brothers. He had faced scary attacks by bears and lions. He never backed down.

One time when a giant came hurling insults at his nation, Intrepid David courageously challenged the giant.

Goliath, the Giant was 9 feet, 9 inches tall but Intrepid David who was only a boy, took him on and defeated him in battle (1 Samuel 17). No sophisticated guns, no soldier's suit or armor tanks. Just a sling of one choice stone from an arsenal of five, slung in confidence in the name of the Lord, and Goliath came crashing like a skyscraper hit by an earthquake.

Listen love, If you must grasp gold? If you must have more wins than wishes in life? Then, never be intimidated by the size, sophistication, wit or threats of the enemy.

One way to put fear under check is to remind yourself of whose you are and who you serve! Intrepid David knew he belonged to the LIVING GOD. Do you know who you belong to?

17

BE VIGILANT

Never neglect details. When everyone's mind is dulled or distracted the leader must be doubly vigilant- Colin Powell

During this time, none of us—not I, nor my relatives, nor my servants, nor the guards who were with me—ever took off our clothes. We carried our weapons with us at all times, even when we went for water. Nehemiah 4:23 (NLT)

Laxity is the reason many callings, dreams and visions come under the enemy's attack. When God commissions you to build a thing, you better anticipate the enemy's vengeful unleash.

A vigilant person keeps careful watch for possible danger or difficulties. Vigilance entails being observant, keen-eyed and on the lookout for possibilities.

God had provided for Nehemiah and his men. They had everything required to rebuild the wall of Jerusalem. Nehemiah trusted in the Lord. He knew how powerful God is. He even petitioned God about the enemies of the vision; yet Nehemiah didn't undermine Sanballat's threat. He and the Men had their weapons on at all times- while working and even when they needed to go for water.

From Nehemiah's display of vigilance, we learn that

Prayers don't replace actions

There is a divine role and a hominal role required for the fulfillment of your dreams.

God and His angels are responsible for the divine but you and I responsible for the hominal. This is why prayers don't replace actions. They make our actions effective for God to use.

God could either prevent or permit an attack

While God could **prevent** Sanballat and Tobias from carrying out their threats? He also could **permit** them to make a move against Nehemiah and His men (Of course just so He can show off his awesome power. I love it when He does.

Nehemiah understood these possibilities hence, he prepared for an attack, knowing that if God didn't prevent Sanballat, he definitely needed a ready human army by which He would destroy the enemy. Rather than sit idly saying God forbid, do this next thing;

<u>Set up a system to guard your gate</u>
Where does desire stir?
Where does your wish dance?
Where are your visions and dreams conceived?
It is all in the heart. Your heart is the gate to your life. You receive information into your heart and by your heart, produce the quality of life you live.

The quality of what you take into your heart determines what you reproduce in all seven dimensions of your life which we discussed in chapter 11- Spiritual, Social, Mental. Career, Financial, Physical and Ministerial.

"Guard your heart above all else, for it determines the course of your life" Proverbs 4:23 (NLT)"

Every negative or positive seed thought reaches for your heart. You have to be your own watch man. Your Sanballat and Tobias may not be humans. They could be circumstances challenging the truth of God's promises over any of the seven dimensions of your life. They could be a crisis threatening to break your marriage, ruin your business and ministry or rob you off the platform God has given you.

In any way, form, shape, manner or colour that Sanballat and Tobias shows up, your job is to guard your heart with all vigilance. Keep your heart free of bitterness, free of anxiety, free of hopelessness so that you can finish the good thing your hands have started building.

1 Peter 5:8 says, *"Stay alert! Watch out for your great enemy, the devil. He prowls around like a roaring lion, looking for someone to devour."*

Don't let that someone be your children. Don't let it be your spouse and most importantly, don't let that someone be the dreams God has planted inside of you.

What system have you set up to protect your heart from the enemy's invasion?

THE 7 WATCH-SYSTEMS OF A PRODUCTIVE HEART

Retained instruction

Any time you are given directions or told how to do something, you are receiving instruction.

Sometimes instruction come directly from the Holyspirt, the written word (bible) or other matured or experienced people. Productive hearts don't only receive instruction they retain it.

"He taught me also, and said unto me, Let thine heart retain my words: keep my commandments, and live."
Proverbs 4:4 (KJB)

Affinity with Wisdom

"Do not forsake wisdom, and she will protect you; love her, and she will watch over you." Proverbs 4:6 (NIV)

Wisdom is both a person and a virtue.

WISDOM AS A PERSON

As a Person, wisdom is Christ.
But to those called by God to salvation, both Jews and Gentiles, Christ is the power of God and the wisdom of God.
1 Corinthians 1:24 (NLT)
The Hebrew word for wisdom (Sophia) means skill. It's used to describe skill in war, art, craftsmanship.
Wisdom is Christ-empowered skill to live for the glory of God. We cannot live wisely without him. His cross, His resurrection, His Holy Spirit empowering us is the only way we can be truly wise.[1]

To have affinity with wisdom is to listen to Christ way more than we listen to our humanness, circumstances and the echoes of darkness' threat.
In Proverbs 8:6, Wisdom (Jesus says), *"Listen to me! For I have important things to tell you. Everything I say is right"* (NLT). Christ's voice is the voice of wisdom and can be found in the pages of the bible and the nudging of the Holy spirit which we sense in the corners of our heart.

WISDOM AS A VIRTUE

Virtue is a behaviour showing high moral standards. As a

virtue, wisdom has seven pillars. These pillars are the foundations of Life, business, marriage and leadership success.

"I, wisdom, dwell together with prudence; I possess knowledge and discretion. To fear the LORD is to hate evil;
I hate pride and arrogance, evil behavior and perverse speech. Counsel and sound judgment are mine; I have insight, I have power. By me kings reign and rulers issue decrees that are just; by me princes govern, and nobles—all who rule on earth. Proverbs 8:12-16(NIV).

- Prudence: A sensible and careful attitude that makes you avoid unnecessary risks.[3]
- Knowledge: Facts, information, and skills acquired through experience or education; the theoretical or practical understanding of a subject.[4]
- Discretion: The quality of behaving or speaking in such a way as to avoid causing offence or revealing confidential information.[5]
- Counsel:Instruction given in directing the judgment or conduct of another.[6]
- Sound judgment: The capacity to assess situations or circumstances shrewdly and to draw sound conclusions.[7]
- Insight: The ability to have a clear deep, and sometimes sudden understanding of a complicated problem or situation.[8]
- Power: the capacity or ability to direct or influence the

behaviour of others or the course of events.[9]

To have affinity with wisdom is to commit to the influence and guidance of the above seven pillars of wisdom as a virtue.

Screened path

Don't do as the wicked do, and don't follow the path of evildoers. Don't even think about it; don't go that way. Turn away and keep moving. Proverbs 4:14-15 (NLT)

Living in a world where evil seems to thrive, you may be tempted to walk in unrighteousness just because you see evil men appearing to prosper. Productive hearts are people who truly win, watch and screen their paths. They understand the difference between good and bad success.

Mark out a straight path for your feet; stay on the safe path. Don't get sidetracked; keep your feet from following evil. Proverbs 4:26-27 (NLT)

Sterilized conversations

Avoid all perverse talk; stay away from corrupt speech. Proverbs 4:24 (NLT)

Your conversations are like an image in a mirror. They reflect the hearts of the people conversing and they project into the hearts of the people conversing. Therefore a conversation is an exchange of spirits. If you are interested in wining on an above average scale, closely guard and sterilize your conversations.

Obscene stories, foolish talk, and coarse jokes-these are not for you. Instead, let there be thankfulness to God.
Ephesians 5:4(NLT)

Purged Company

Do not be misled: "Bad company corrupts good character."
1 Corinthians 15:33 (NIV)

Emmanuel James "Jim" Rohn an American entrepreneur, author and motivational speaker said, "You are the average of the five people you spend the most time with."
  When people quote Jim, their minds quickly scan their network of friends, colleagues, mentors and coaches. While those are involved in the five if you spend much time with them, the one person you will definitely spend the most time with is the person you eventually marry.

If you are single? It means you have the chance to choose right. Please ensure that your spouse is the kind of person you want to become. They should have virtues that you will like to see grow in your life and of course in the lives of your children. If you marry a liar, you are going to someday have to lie for them. That makes you a liar too. If you marry someone without integrity, you are going to have to compromise to keep peace.

Closely watch the people you spend time with over the phone or physically. If bad company corrupts good manners? Good company strengthens gold wins.

Fixed eyes

Look straight ahead, and fix your eyes on what lies before you. Proverbs 4:25 (NLT)

Do you have a vision ? Are you headed somewhere in life? How do you want to arrive at your desired destination? Would you want to arrive broken, weak, discouraged and defeated or would you rather arrive strong, fit, whole and in charge? It is up to you.

You are going to have many beasts try to stop you. You are going to see several pits of snakes covered with inviting linen. Please don't stop to admire or take a rest on it. Look straight ahead until you arrive at where God is calling you. Jealously protect your vision. Protect your focus no matter what or who hits you.

Weighing mind

Ponder the path of thy feet, and let all thy ways be established. Proverbs 4:26(KJB)

The only time impulse is guaranteed to favour you is when

you have to quickly escape from danger. Other than that, impulse always leaves you with something to regret about. Practice weighing the pros and cons of every option life or anyone presents you. Never go by the first impression, the first look, the first suggestion, the first nudge, the first set of options, the first desire. Analyze and weigh what's before you. A weighing mind is proof of vigilance.

18

BE EQUIPPED

The extent to which you are equipped for the mission is totally up to you. Never leave anything to chance- Anne Atulaegwu

The laborers carried on their work with one hand supporting their load and one hand holding a weapon. All the builders had a sword belted to their side. Nehemiah 4:17-18 (NLT)

I am thrilled by Nehemiah's display of wisdom on this wall

project. He made each builder carry a sword on one hand while they built with the other.

Just in case you are wondering how heavy a sword was at the time, Leading sword expert Ewart Oakeshott stated: "Medieval Swords are neither unwieldably heavy nor all alike. The average weight of any one of normal size is between 2.5 lbs and 3.5 lbs.[1]"

2.5lbs is roughly 1kg. That is about the mass of a little water bottle or one loaf and a half of bread. Clearly, it wasn't impossible for the men to hold their swords on one hand and build with the other.

Like Nehemiah did for his men, God has already provided all you need for possible battles but It is up to you to be equipped for the mission. For instance, The men could have dropped their swords in a "safe place" intending to pick it up when Sanballat and his army strikes but they chose to hold their swords in readiness for an attack.

As builders in the kingdom, our sword is of the spirit. It is light weight, sharp and effective. It is the word of God. *"And take the helmet of salvation, and the sword of the Spirit, which is the word of God: Ephesians 6:17 (KJB)"* God has given us His word, it is up to us to use it!

From Nehemiah's men we learn that the word of God which is our sword should be ready on our lips and heart at all times. We already know that the enemy can attack at any time. This knowledge doesn't make us abandon the mission in fear, neither do we ignore the possibility of an attack. Rather we wield the sword of the spirit consistently while building that which has been assigned to us.

When you sense a possible attack in any area of your life, wield your sword! Wield it over your reputation, resolution and results.

19

BE ATTENTIVE

The Lord always signals the believer. How much we discern is dependent on our attentiveness- Anne Atulaegwu

*When you hear the blast of the trumpet,
rush to wherever it is sounding.
Then our God will fight for us!" Nehemiah 4:20 (NLT)*

The blast of a trumpet was notably Israel's alarm system. A trumpet was blown when they needed to assemble on different occasions and for various purposes such as announcing a jubilee, the coronation of a king, praising God, calling the army to war and inducing fear within the hearts of enemy soldiers.

Nehemiah asked the men to listen for the trumpet because it was the signal required for them to enter war mode.

As believers, the Lord signals us with sounds too. Do you listen for these sounds? Can you interpret the sound signals that your spirit man is picking up?

In the business of your everyday life, dare to listen for the sounds of God. Sometimes, He notifies you to pray, to withdraw from a person or situation, to reject an offer, to re-negotiate a deal, to love on that boss who despitefully uses you, to abstain from your favourite TV program, to stay some more in His arms during your quiet time. Do you yield? Or do you allow the noise of this world to deafen you?

Sound signals are also God's way of announcing the seasons of our lives to us. Perhaps, you can recall a time when everyone around you appeared to say a particular word or phrase that meant nothing to them but struck you significantly. You may have tried to overlook it as mere coincidence when eventually, you start hearing same word or phrase on TV or radio or read the word or phrase in a book. Such things are not coincidental they are actually sound signals for you in that season.

Also, you may have experienced songs playing in your heart which you didn't recently listen to. At times they are songs of consolation, sometimes songs of warfare and other times songs of adoration to God. The Holy spirit speaks to us through music in our souls.

I have also heard people say whenever they find that they are singing burial hymns or songs, they soon get news that someone they know have passed on.

 Beyond sounds, God speaks to us in diverse ways. Some of the ways by which God speaks to us are;

An Inner witness:

We usually call it "something in me". You've probably heard people say things like "something in me told me to leave that place." That "something in you" could be God's voice urging you to escape danger. This inner witness is sometimes called a conscience. An example of God's voice in man's conscience can be seen in 1 Samuel 24:5.

David had cut Saul's garment whilst Saul slept because he wanted Saul to know that he (David) wasn't interested in killing him. Although his intention seemed good, God rebuked him through his conscience. 1 Samuel 24:5-7

An audible voice: God sometimes speaks loud enough for our physical ears to hear. An example would be when He called Samuel in 1 Samuel 3. Samuel thought it was Eli and so he went to Eli. Samuel could think it was Eli because God spoke audibly for his physical ears to hear.

Dreams/ Visions: There are times when a graphical representation is required for a message to clearly get to the receiver. God could use dreams (motion pictures captured in a sleep) or visions (motion pictures captured while one is awake). A popular example would be Joseph and the dreams about God's plan for his future, when he saw that his parents and siblings bowed to him (Genesis 37)

<u>Silence</u>: There are times when God says a lot just by keeping silent. He sometimes speaks this way when he disapproves of our chosen path and is unwilling to force us to do the right thing. This certainly is after he has warned us clearly. An example would be a time in Israel's history when God's voice/word became scarce. The people had gone their own ways and God was unhappy with them. (1 Samuel 3:1)

<u>The written word of God</u>: This is the bible. The bible contains the mind of God over every situation in life. The word is the accepted yardstick against which we judge any voice we hear. One mistake most people make is to judge a voice based on how it makes them feel. Even though the voice of God brings peace to our hearts, God's voice can also cause an unrest in order to spur us towards obedience. Likewise, the voice of the devil can bring temporal relief to spur us to disobey God's word. Therefore, deciphering voices have nothing to do with feelings but faith in God's word (The BIBLE).

"Dear friends, do not believe every spirit, but test the spirits to see whether they are from God" 1 John 4:1 (NIV)

If a voice says anything contrary to what is in the bible. Then it can't be the voice of God. God will never contradict His word. He is not the author of confusion. (1 Corinthians 14:33).

Pay close attention to signals and the word of God. It will help you decipher the seasons and move of God for, in and through your life per time.

HOW TO TELL THE DIFFERENCE BETWEEN GOD'S VOICE AND YOUR MIND

I believe that the voice of God is instilled in everyone at creation. And Like Adam who heard God's voice after He and his wife sinned, God speaks to everyone – the sinner and the righteous. Unfortunately, man is always searching for the voice of God because sin which brought separation between man and God, has shrouded God's voice in so much noise that we struggle to tell His voice from those of others and even our own minds.

Despite the confusion, God continues to speak and desperately longs for us to hear his voice more than we want to. The first step to knowing God's voice is to **have a relationship with Him**.

This relationship begins when we acknowledge, confess aloud and believe in our hearts that JESUS is God's Son, that He died for our sins, was buried and now lives forever (Romans 10:9). When this happens, we enter into an intimate fellowship with God the father, through His son and His Holy spirit who comes to live inside our bodies. (1 John 1:3).

This priceless relationship requires us to spend time getting to know God. He already knows us, so we need to know Him. Our knowledge of Him will bring us to a place of our own true identity- when we consistently show forth his glory and praise.

Knowing God's voice is one of the many beautiful knowledge of Him that we possess as we spend time with him in prayer, studying His word and walking in consistent obedience.

In the original plan, our minds were to be one with God's mind. In fact when God made Adam, it was so. Adam was created in God's image and likeness (Genesis 1:27). Adam had the mind of God. When Adam named an animal Dog, Cat or horse; it was exactly what God had in mind for them to be called.

Things were in order until Adam fell. It became difficult to know God's mind or will in an instant. Like Adam we now have to earnestly seek God's mind/will/voice.

BUT, a **restoration order was set up**!

The order was such that if anyone enters into a relationship with God through Jesus Christ His son, He was restored into the image of God. This means that individual receives and has the mind of Christ/God.

"For who hath known the mind of the Lord, that he may instruct him? But we have the mind of Christ." 1 Corinthians

2:16 (KJB)

However, we notice that our old way of thinking keeps getting in the way. We are saddled with the responsibility of aligning with our new, original mind of Christ or the old mind of the flesh.

To successfully live in alignment with our new, authentic mind, Apostle Paul advices us to renew our minds. *"And be not conformed to this world: but be ye transformed by the renewing of your mind, that ye may prove what is that good, and acceptable, and perfect, will of God." Romans 12:2(KJB)*

WHAT IT MEANS TO RENEW YOUR MIND

The renewal of the mind is a deliberate constant effort to
1. Be aware of God's word concerning a situation
2. Meditate on God's word until we grasp its truth
3. Walk in obedience to God's word irrespective of how our bodies feel.

In simpler terms, your mind is renewed in knowledge, meditation and obedience to the word.

When your mind is renewed, you will no longer worry if it is "your mind" that is speaking to you or the "mind of God"; because a renewed mind is one with God and therefore, it is the mind of God.

So how can a believer tell if information is his own thoughts or the voice of God within HIM?

Judge the information from the voice against the word of God. If it tallies? That is God. If it contradicts? it might be you or a strange voice.

However, there are situations that are matters of decision making/choice. Such situations may not be expressly found in God's word. A good example would be seeking God's thought/will concerning what course you should enroll for at the university.

In this case, you should ask the Lord to make His will known to you. God would either speak to you in any of the ways we talked about earlier or He could use someone or even a situation or your interests to reveal His will concerning issues like that. The most important thing to remember when deciphering God's voice is this: GOD'S VOICE WILL NEVER PUT YOU INTO A STATE OF CONFUSION.

20

BE WHOLE HEARTED

We were not sent into this world to do anything into which we cannot put our heart- John Ruskin

So we rebuilt the wall till all of it reached half its height, for the people worked with all their heart. Nehemiah 4:6 (NIV)

Wholeheartedness is the quality of being completely and sincerely devoted, determined, enthusiastic and free from hesitation.[1]

Nehemiah and the Jews were unreservedly committed to

the project. This made them work consistently form sunrise to sunset. *"We worked early and late, from sunrise to sunset."* Nehemiah 4:21 (NIV)

Commitment is a proof of wholeheartedness; wholeheartedness is the proof of value.

How much do you value your relationship with God?

Do you value your mission?

How valuable is your purpose to you?

Is your vision of any worth to you?

If you value these things, you will give your whole heart to its course and fulfillment.

One major reason people are on and off about their missions is because their hearts are divided. They are torn between the pleasures of their comfort zones and the pain/price demanded by their missions.

I have noticed that wholeheartedness towards the mission God has assigned to you, is directly proportional to your wholeheartedness towards God. When you start having divided attention towards God, your commitment towards the mission equally drops.

SIGNS OF A DIVIDED HEART

Matt White founder at ELITE Leadership Bible Institute and Senior Pastor at Calvary Worship Center, USA reveals the following as signs of a divided heart.

<u>You are no longer clingy</u>

Romans 12:9(NIV) says, "*Love must be sincere. Hate what is evil; cling to what is good.*"
You've given in to pet sins and old patterns of unbelief and sin. You're no longer clinging to what is good and in some areas of your life you've relaxed your grip and let the world's ways rule.

You've lost the fizz

You could easily describe your relationship with God as flat. In reality, you've lost your first love. The passion and pop have been replaced with routine and a list of to do's. The Bible calls this lukewarmness. We talked about it in chapter 10. This is a dangerous place to be. Jesus rebuked the church in Ephesus for losing their fizz in Revelation 2:4 (NIV) "But *I have this against you, that you have left your first love*".

People are annoying

You get easily irritated by other people's shortcomings. Lately your mantra has been, "If it's going to be done right it's going to have to be me." The person ahead of you in the checkout line has too many items. The car in front of you is too slow. The first sign of a heart losing its devotion to God is a heart that has no time or patience for the people around them.

You're too busy to pray

Even when you want to, know you need to, you don't have

the time to pray. When you do, you do so in haste. Prayerlessness is proof of tampered devotion.

<u>You've got no time to serve</u>

A heart fully devoted to God looks for ways to express that devotion through service. The less you want to serve God through acts of compassion, ministry and simple acts of good deeds, the more your heart has grown distant from the God who gave His all.

WHAT TO DO WHEN YOUR HEART IS DIVIDED

Teach me your way, LORD, that I may rely on your faithfulness; give me an undivided heart, that I may fear your name. Psalms 86:11(NIV)

<u>Admit it</u>

The enemy has a way of tricking our minds to believe we are still standing so long as we are not flat on the ground yet. Slipping off is one second different from falling. Hence, Paul wasn't holding water in his mouth when he said, *"let he that thinks he stands take heed lest he falls."* 1 Corinthians 10:12(KJB). Admit that your purpose no longer has your whole attention. Admit that God no longer has all of your loyalty. Admit that a part of you is longing for and running after mammon. Admit that you need help.

<u>Blow the whistle</u>

Let your soul know who is in charge now. Decide that you

are done chasing the wind or living one leg in an one leg outside God's purpose for you. You are going to partner with God to build what He wants to build in, through, and for you. Decide that you will no longer be disloyal to God and your purpose.

Repent

Truth is a divided heart is a sin. *"'You must love the LORD your God with all your heart, all your soul, all your strength, and all your mind" Luke 10:27 (NLT)*
Get real with God. He is so loving and will forgive if you sincerely ask him to forgive you and forsake that which you apologized for. *"If we confess our sins, he is faithful and just to forgive us our sins, and to cleanse us from all unrighteousness. 1 John 1:9 (KJB)*

Shut the door

If Noah didn't shut the door of the ark. What happened to the other people outside the ark would have happened to those in the ark.
Admitting, Deciding, Repenting won't make any difference if you don't intentionally deny (the things that breeds disloyalty) access into your heart. Don't give room for your flesh. Prioritize your relationship with God. Prioritize your mission.

Wholeheartedness is a necessity if you are serious about grabbing gold. I understand that you don't mean for your heart to be divided. Life happens and things don't always go as you wish but you can always turn your wishes into wins if you master your heart and refuse to sway with the tides.

6 HEART CONDITIONS TO GUARD AGAINST

When I was a child, I believed everything. I believed my father was the strongest man on earth. I believed God could truly do all things. I was surely sure that God was able to handle anything.

As I grew older, I experienced moments of failure, uncertainty, disappointment and a whole lot of not so good drama. I'm pretty sure you can relate with that too.
You know what honey? It's okay to cry in moments like that but dangerous to let those experiences influence your heart.

The heart is the citadel of power. It determines a whole lot than we actually know. Scripture says in Proverbs 4:23," Guard your heart **above all else**, for it determines the course of your life'. (NLT) emphasis added.
It says ABOVE ALL ELSE guard your heart. Why would guarding the heart be top priority? **It's because the heart determines all else.**

The heart is so important that it is the first thing God changes when we encounter Him at the point of salvation. Ezekiel 36:26
Where do you feel joy?
Where do you feel pain?
Where do you feel love?
Where do you feel conviction?
Where do you feel numb?

THE HEART!

Although a cold person might claim to feel nothing; He definitely feels cold.

The ability of the heart to feel is what processes our experiences and the result of that process sets the course of our life.

I remember having been through an excruciating heartbreak many years back. I was shattered in many several shades of the word- shattered. I laid before the Lord crying and I kept saying, "I love you Christ but trust me we are no longer going to do these things your way. Feel free to lead me in other areas but this one because you've failed me real bad."

Have you ever spoken to God bluntly?

I did during those times.

Oh how I love the Lord.

He didn't bark at me. He didn't push me off. He just said," **Annie, don't let the experience change your heart because if it does, you would have given it the permission to direct the rest of your life and you won't love the outcome. It was just an event. One you should grow from not one to define you."**

Need I say my perspective changed immediately? The Lord loved me through that dark season of my life and here I am today a better, prettier Princess (Laughs)

All of life's experiences are targeted towards the heart because the heart is the real deal.

I understand that your dad never bought the bicycle he

promised since you were two years old. Don't allow that experience influence you to doubt every time God makes a promise.

Perhaps you tried a business one time and you fell flat on your face and so you've become crippled by fear of failure?

Could it be that Life has beaten you so bad that disappointment has become your surname and made you go about hopelessly?

May I remind you that experiences are meant to **grow** and not **go** us. You should still be on stage after the famine, hurt, and what not rolls off.

If you truly want to live out the best God has for you. If you want to fulfill the Assignment on your life, if you really want to turn your wishes into wins and see your dreams go from paper to play out, then you must guard against these six heart diseases/conditions.

The fearful heart:

Fear is one of the cruelest torments one could ever experience. Perhaps you fear that the past might catch up with you, that the present would never be as desired or that the future hasn't got the slightest chance at becoming.

I need you to know that your fears can never be more powerful than your faith in God. Therefore you must decide to counter those fear streams with oceans of faith in God and His powerful ability at work in you, through you and for you. Be reminded of God's word in Isaiah 35:4 *"Say to those with fearful hearts, "Be strong, and do not fear, for your God is coming to destroy your enemies. He is coming to save you."*

The double minded heart:
It's pretty easy to move from full lights on faith to not being so sure that our dreams will manifest especially when we decide to entertain negative pictures or suggestions.
The double minded heart makes you unrecognizable before God. This is why Apostle James says such person shouldn't think they would receive anything from God-James 1:8.
It makes one unstable and instability is the reason some people can't pull through a project from start to finish. Others have many incomplete projects and keep starting new ones which they soon abandon to start another new one. A double minded heart robs you off the joy of fulfillment. It makes you retrogress when you ought to be far ahead in your pack. Don't let your heart catch this bug.
Fix your thoughts on the ability of God in you. Never forget that He is way bigger than our minds can fathom.

The hopeless heart:
Sometimes it's really difficult to keep hope alive especially when you've been though disappointment repeatedly. I need you to remember sweetheart, that yesterday's rain doesn't negate today/tomorrow's sunshine. Keep your hope alive no matter how bad it gets in your storyline!
Remember Proverbs 23:18(KJV) *"For surely there is an end; and thine expectation shall not be cut off.*

The Hardened Heart:

We tend to get this kind of heart when we've been offended. Scripture says *"a brother wronged is more unyielding than a fortified city"* Proverbs 18:19.

Even though the unyieldingness in this verse refers to relationships with other humans, we can also become unyielding /hardened towards God when we get offended by Him, by our church, by spiritual leaders or anything connected to our faith.

The danger posed by this heart is that it has the capacity to annihilate our next good season.

You must guard your heart from offences. Apostle Paul says *Watch out that no poisonous root of bitterness grows up to trouble you, corrupting many"* Hebrews 12:15 (NLT).

Bitterness and offence precedes hardness of heart. Protect yourself from being defiled by them.

The Anxious Heart:

Personally I have noticed that whenever my heart falls into this state, the Lord warns me by opening my eyes in a night dream or a day-vision. I'll see myself walking around barefooted. For years I didn't understand until one day when it seemed like an every night dream. I became deeply concerned and I asked Him. The scripture He dropped in my heart was Ephesians 6:15 (KJV*) "and with your feet fitted with the readiness that comes from the gospel of peace."*

Then the Lord said, "**The gospel of peace is simple. It is the truth that when you cast your burden on me, I truly lift them off so you don't have to keep moving about with**

it. I am your rest Annie. I still don't see what you're anxious about when I already got the issue fixed the first moment you asked for my help" My eyes popped.

He said anxiety makes me unready to receive what I've prayed for and exposes me to Satan's attack.

I looked up several other translations, every commentary available on that verse and I saw clearly that I indeed heard the Lord.

Anxiety is proof that you doubt the strength of God. It keeps you restless and you can't effectively defend the territories assigned to you. It also stops you from conquering new frontiers.

I have sat up on this one, using the approaches I shared with you in chapter 5. I encourage you to step up too.

The Simple Heart:

This sounds good but is a huge danger to one's purpose or dreams. The word simple refers to one who believes every word, is easily enticed or easily swayed by other people's convictions.

I used to be this way in the past. In fact I once dated someone who lied to me repeatedly and got angry I wasn't picking it such that he called me gullible. I mean he was a "highly placed" believer and I didn't think he would comfortably lie about anything and so I trusted without waiting for time to reveal who he really was. Don't blame me, I was only 19 at the time. (Laughs)

Many young people are like that. We think the world sees things through our eyes. If only we knew that it isn't so. This heart condition leaves us broken, hurting, sometimes confused and perhaps angry at life because our simple heart keeps driving us to the face of unending disappointment.

Scripture says that the cure for a simple heart is wisdom. *"O simple ones, **learn prudence**; O fools, learn sense."* Proverbs 8:5 (ESV).

Prudence is a branch/pillar of wisdom. The Hebrew word for prudence in that verse is "ormah" [1] and is translated as subtlety!

The enemy wants us to believe that being subtle is evil. Well it isn't. If it were? God wouldn't have made the serpent subtle. God creates no evil and so if he made the serpent the most subtle of them all (Genesis 3:1), it means that subtlety is a skill-one which is very important.

In fact, Genesis 3:1 explains that all the animals God made had some measure of subtlety but the serpent was the most subtle. Please do not mistake this skill for being manipulative. Manipulation and subtlety are not the same.

Subtlety means having or showing skill at recognizing and understanding things that are not obvious. Manipulation means controlling someone or something to your own advantage, often unfairly or dishonestly.

From the above, we see that subtlety can't possibly be evil or be associated with the devil.

Proverbs 22: 3(NLT) says *"A **prudent** person foresees danger and takes precautions. The **simpleton** goes blindly on and suffers the consequences."* You can see that the cure for simple heart is prudence (a pillar of wisdom). Apostle James says *"if any of you lack wisdom, just ask!"* James 1:5

Stop letting people take undue advantage of you. Ask God for wisdom to relate with people and train your eyes to recognize situations/people that conceal their intention and capacity to destroy or hurt you.

This is the reason I keep telling young people that there is no such thing as "blind love". Yeah, you should close one eye in marriage as they say but please never do that before you make those vows.

Remember *"The* **simpleton** *goes blindly on and suffers the consequences."* Proverbs 22:3

Prudence secures the glory of your future. Be prudent.

FINAL WORDS

Desires are pathways through which God engages the earth in order to fulfill his plan and purpose amongst men.
- Anne Atulaegwu

Every time God wants to do something on earth, He plants the desire for that thing in the heart of a man or a group of people. This desire becomes yearnings or longings of the soul of that man or group of people, such that they are moved to do things that will trigger the move of God in the direction He (God) plans.

For instance, In Judges 14, Samson desired a philistine woman as wife. This was shocking to his parents and they disapproved of the marriage considering that Israelites were forbidden to marry from other nations.

"You must not intermarry with them. Do not let your daughters and sons marry their sons and daughters, for they will lead your children away from me to worship other gods. Then the anger of the LORD will burn against you, and he will quickly destroy you." Deuteronomy 7:3-4 (NLT)

In this case, Samson's desire wasn't because He had no respect for God's instruction. It was God himself, who wanted an opportunity to confront the Philistines so that He could destroy them through Samson.

"His father and mother replied, "Isn't there an acceptable woman among your relatives or among all our people? Must you go to the uncircumcised Philistines to get a wife?" But Samson said to his father, "Get her for me. She's the right one for me." His parents did not know that this was from the LORD, who was seeking an occasion to confront the Philistines; for at that time they were ruling over Israel.) Judges 14:3-4 (NLT)

When you read through chapters 14 and 15, you will see that the Lord indeed used that desire to deal with the philistines who oppressed Israel at the time.

Another Instance is the occasion of great revivals on the earth. Every revival was preceded by the earnest prayer of a man or group of people in whom the Lord had stirred the desire for a revival.

How does this concern you?

If desires are pathways through which God engages the earth, it means not every desire in your heart is a coincidence.

You have to be sensitive enough to decipher why you strongly wish for something. I encourage you to be a man or woman of prayer and depths of intimacy with God. Consistently bring your heart before the Lord in prayer and ask Him to align your desires/wishes with His. Only then can you truly win because the real wins in life are not in the ephemeral possessions or achievements that we are privileged to grasp while on earth. The real wins occur when our souls grasp, nurture and manifest the desires of God upon the earth.

If you do not have a personal relationship with Jesus Christ yet, I encourage you to do so. Follow the steps below to a personal relationship with God.

- Accept the fact that you were born a sinner and no amount of good can make you right with God except the blood of Jesus.
- Confess your position and acts as a sinner.
- Surrender to the Lordship of Christ.
- Identify and commit to the ways of Christ in a local church.

Please say this prayer with me if you are ready to let Jesus lead and rule in your life.

Lord Jesus, I Confess That I Am A Sinner. I Believe That You Died To Pay For My Sins And You Rose From The Dead Giving Me Victory Over Sin And Death.

I Surrender To Your Lordship Over My Life. Forgive Me, Wash And Sanctify Me By Your Blood. Give Me Your Holyspirit That I May Live For You.

By Faith, I Receive Your Forgiveness. I Therefore Confess With My Mouth And Believe In My Heart That Jesus Is My Lord And Saviour.

I Confess That I Am The Righteousness Of God In Christ Jesus. I Receive Your Spirit To Dwell In My Heart From This Day Onward, Amen.

ANNE ATULAEGWU

ABOUT THE AUTHOR

Princess Anne Atulaegwu is an inspiring personality with a huge passion to see YOU live fulfilled. She is a conference convener, speaker, youth coach, counselor, Mentor and teacher.

Anne specializes in birthing God's purpose in the heart of young people, teaching them to nurse their vision and prophetically empowering them to fulfill destiny.

In the past 18 years, she has mentored and raised teens\youths from desolation into amazing destinies. She loves to be with them and throws in her all for their best to manifest.Anne holds Bachelor's in agricultural Education from the University of Nigeria, Nsukka.

ANNE ATULAEGWU

She holds a diploma in ministerial counseling and a bachelor's degree in theology and Christian Education respectively from Faith College of Arts and Theology (FACAT), Lagos. She is a Chaplain from International institute of pastoral Education and Chaplaincy (IIPEC), Ogun state.

She is a certified NLP practitioner and currently training towards certification as a Life Purpose Coach.

She is the founder of The Birth Place Fulfillment Foundation; a youth and women focused ministry with the mandate to raise a generation of passionate young people and women who establish God's purpose in every facet of life through conferences, seminars and mentoring.

Anne is an author, psalmist, songwriter, poet and a great dancer.

Possessing an infectious passion for Christ and love for people, she excellently combines insights from scriptures, neuro-linguistic programming, positive psychology and behavioural science in her practice as a counselor, mentor, coach and teacher.

She lives in Lagos, Nigeria; where she currently serves as a youth pastor in her local assembly-Abundant House of Grace, INC.

CONNECT WITH ANNE

Interested in getting Anne to speak at your youth or teen event? Contact us at **www.anneatulaegwu.com**

Connect with Anne on social media

Facebook: **@anneatulaegwu**

Instagram**:@anneatulaegwu**

Twitter: **@AtulaegwuAnne**

Subscribe to her Youtube channel for weekly inspiration**: https://www.youtube.com/c/anneatulaegwuTV**

To read poems on purpose, love and life go to

http://www.insyncwithpurpose.blogspot.com Join over 1000 young women on Tamar's Pouch facebook group

https://www.facebook.com/groups/tamarspouch

OTHER BOOKS BY ANNE

All available at www.anneatulaegwu.com

PROTHESIS... An Exposition on your destiny

In the book **Prothesis** you will:

- Learn details about God's perfect design for your life.

- Learn to let God lead you into His flawless purpose for you.
- Understand the link between your gifts/talents and your purpose.
- Understand the power and purpose of a personal covenant with God Learn to walk in obedience to God's direction
- Get powerful glimpses into your destiny
- Be empowered to make your mark, be relevant and live fulfilled.

This book challenges you to move from where you are to where you ought to be - a glorious fulfilling life! Join me on a journey to fulfillment.

TAMAR....Breaking off the shackles of abuse

In TAMAR, Anne tells the epic story of three women whose names bonded them-TAMAR.

Raped by a brother, Denied by her father-in-law and raised by an abused aunt respectively, all three women aptly represent the various forms of abuse faced by men and women in our societies today.

Buried in its pages is lasting freedom from all forms of abuse- physical, emotional, financial and even spiritual!

Relevant to men and women.

7 SIGNS YOU ARE SABOTAGING YOUR LIFE.. and how to rescue to it

In this book, Anne interestingly shows you

- 7 warning signs that you might be ruining all you are currently working for.
- Helps you identify the triggers associated with self sabotaging behaviours.

- Leads you to a productive place of self awareness for increased productivity and better relationships.
- Exposes practical approaches to dealing with habits such as lies, haste, excessive love of pleasure, impulsive spending, slothfulness/Laziness, Lose/Leaking mouth and stinginess.
- Empowers you to GET BACK ALL you've ignorantly or mistakenly ruined.

Love your future? Read this fast.

EXECUTIVE SUMMIT (VOLUME 1)

Living in times when days fly by fast, technology gets upgraded per second and last night's most trendy dress takes the back seat by morning; we sure need some stability for our souls without losing touch with the times.

If you've ever desired a richer, fuller life that includes material blessings and the true riches of eternal worth? Then you must become wise- a person who heeds instruction.

In the Executive summit series, Anne Atulaegwu serves you a good doze of stability and wisdom required for you to live fulfilled, make you mark where it matters most and retain relevance in an ever changing world.

NOTES

CHAPTER 1

1. Conquering fear: An Ethopian folktale
   https://www.uexpress.com/tell-me-a-

story/2011/10/23/conquering-fear-an-ethiopian-folktale (accessed 30th october 2018)

2. https://en.wikipedia.org/wiki/Fear (accessed 10th march 2017)

3. Perceptionhttps://en.oxforddictionaries.com/definition/perception (accessed 10th march 2017)

4. https://www.dictionary.com/browse/fear (accessed 10th march 2017)

CHAPTER 3

1. Arnold Lobel, "Tomorrow" Days with Frog and Toad https://www.reddit.com/r/getdisciplined/comments/1v2par/this_childrens_story_from_frog_and_toad_contains/ (accessed 30th October 2018)

CHAPTER 4

1. Anne Atulaegwu(2009) Distraction https://www.anneatulaegwu.com/2009/07/distractions_13.html
 (accessed 30th October 2018)

2. Focus https://dictionary.cambridge.org/dictionary/english/focus (accessed 24th September 2016)

CHAPTER 5

1. *365 Devotions,* Standard Publishing http://ministry127.com/resources/illustration/flying-in-the-clouds (accessed 21st November 2018)

2. https://en.oxforddictionaries.com/definition/anxiety (accessed 21st November 2018)

3. https://www.hhs.gov/answers/mental-health-and-substance-abuse/what-are-the-five-major-types-of-anxiety-disorders/index.html (accessed 21st November 2018)

4. https://en.wikipedia.org/wiki/Anxiety#cite_note-WHO2009-6 (accessed 21st November 2018)

5. https://en.wikipedia.org/wiki/Anxiety#cite_note-TestaGiannuzzi2013partI-9 (accessed 21st November 2018)

6. https://en.wikipedia.org/wiki/Anxiety (accessed 21st November 2018)

7. https://www.healthline.com/health/anxiety/anxiety-triggers (accessed 21st November 2018)

8. Spaghetti body, Child and Adolescent Psychology http://theplumtree.net/wp-content/uploads/2016/01/Spaghetti-Body.pdf (accessed 21st November 2018)

9. STRESS QUIZ: Kohn, P. M., and J. E. MacDonald. 1992. The survey of recent life experiences: A decontaminated hassles scale for adults. Journal of Behavioral Medicine 15:221–236. Copyright © 1992 by Plenum Publishing Corporation. With kind permission of Springer Science and Business Media.

10. Deep Breathing, Child and Adolescent Psychology http://theplumtree.net/wp-content/uploads/2016/01/Deep-Breathing.pdf

CHAPTER 6

1. https//.en.m.wikipedia.org/wiki/Emotion (accessed June 6th 2018)
2. http://biblehub.com/greek/2192.htm (accessed June 6th 2018)
3. http://biblehub.com/greek/4102.htm (accessed June 6th 2018)

CHAPTER 7

1. http://www.anneatulaegwu.com/2016/06/7-choices-you-will-regret-in-7-years.html (accessed June 6th 2018)

CHAPTER 8

1. https://www.livin3.com/5-motivational-and-inspiring-short-stories
2. https://en.wikipedia.org/wiki/Planning
3. http://www.businessdictionary.com/definition/objective.html
4. Barron's Management book fourth edition, Authors: Patrick J. Montana and Bruce H. Charnov
5. Mike Morrision (2011) Difference between goals and objectives https://rapidbi.com/the-difference-between-goals-objectives/

6. _Locke, Edwin A.; Latham, Gary P. (1990). A theory of goal setting & task performance. Englewood Cliffs, NJ: Prentice Hall. ISBN 0139131388. OCLC 20219875._

7. http://www.investorwords.com/article/goals-vs-objectives.html#ixzz5GmHtnse8 (INVESTOR WORDS TABLE)

CHAPTER 9

1. Derek Rydall 2013, The paralysis of over-analysis https://www.huffingtonpost.com/derek-rydall/overanalyzing-_b_3897480.html accessed 24th may 2018

CHAPTER 11

1. Andrea Antoniu; MORAL STORY THAT WILL CHANGE YOUR BAD HABITS https://andreiantoniu.com/moral-story-that-will-change-your-bad-habits/ (accessed on 29th October 2018)

2. Definition of Habit. Merriam Webster Dictionary. Accessed on 29th October 2018

3. Andrews, B. R. (1903). "Habit". The American Journal of Psychology. University of Illinois Press. 14 (2): 121–49. doi:10.2307/1412711. ISSN 0002-9556. JSTOR 1412711 – via JSTOR.

4. Duhigg, C. (n.d.). Retrieved from https://www.npr.org/2012/03/05/147192599/habits-how-they-form-and-how-to-break-them Accessed on 29th October 2018

5. Habits: Why we do what we do; An interview with **Charles Duhigg,** reporter for *The New York Times* and author of *The Power of Habit: Why We Do What We Do in Life and Business.* https://hbr.org/2012/06/habits-why-we-do-what-we-do Accessed on 29th October 2018

6. http://make-or-break-habits.com/why-habits-are-important/ Accessed on 29th October 2018

7. James Clear. The 5 triggers that make new habits stick https://jamesclear.com/habit-triggers Accessed on 29th October 2018

CHAPTER 12

1. Pedro Pablo: My little world has broken https://freestoriesforkids.com/children/stories-and-tales/my-little-world-has-broken (accessed October 29th 2018).

2. Flexibility http://characterfirsteducation.com/c/curriculum-detail/2200969 (accessed October 29th 2018).

CHAPTER 13

1. **G.M Matheny, Heavenly Rewards** https://www.truechristianshortstoriesfreebygmmathen

y.com/heavenly-rewards.html **(accessed 27th November 2018)**

2. https://en.oxforddictionaries.com/definition/reward **(accessed 27th November)**

CHAPTER 14

1. https://en.oxforddictionaries.com/definition/impervious (accessed 12th November 2018)

2. https://www.merriam-webster.com/dictionary/petition (accessed 12th November 2018)

CHAPTER 15

1. https://en.oxforddictionaries.com/definition/thoughtfulness (accessed 12th November 2018)

CHAPTER 16

1. https://www.thefreedictionary.com/intrepid (accessed Novemeber 13th 2018)

Chapter 17

1. https://www.ldoceonline.com/dictionary/prudence (accessed 26th November 2018)

2. https://en.oxforddictionaries.com/definition/knowledge (accessed 26th November 2018)

3. https://en.oxforddictionaries.com/definition/discretion

(accessed 26th November 2018)

4. https://www.dictionary.com/browse/counsel (accessed 26th November 2018)

5.   http://www.webster-dictionary.org/definition/sound+judgement (accessed 26th November 2018)

6. https://dictionary.cambridge.org/dictionary/english/insight (accessed 26th November 2018)

Chapter 18

1. **_J. Clements, "What did Historical Swords Weigh?"_** http://www.thearma.org/essays/weights.htm#.W_vNSThKjIU (accessed 26th November 2018)

CHAPTER 20

1.   http://pastormattwhite.blogspot.com/2016/08/5-signs-of-divided-heart.html(accessed 26th November 2018)